REGGAESTORIES

REGGAE STORIES
Jamaican Musical Legends and Cultural Legacies

EDITED BY
DONNA P. HOPE

The University of the West Indies Press
Jamaica • Barbados • Trinidad and Tobago

The University of the West Indies Press
7A Gibraltar Hall Road, Mona
Kingston 7, Jamaica
www.uwipress.com

© 2018 Donna P. Hope
All rights reserved. Published 2018

A catalogue record of this book is available from the
National Library of Jamaica.

ISBN: 978-976-640-669-1 (print)
978-976-640-670-7 (Kindle)
978-976-640-671-4 (ePub)

Cover and book design by Robert Harris
Set in Minion Pro 11/15 x 24
Printed in the United States of America

The University of the West Indies Press has no responsibility for the persistence or accuracy of URLs for external or third-party Internet websites referred to in this publication and does not guarantee that any content on such websites is, or will remain, accurate or appropriate.

CONTENTS

Acknowledgements *vii*

Introduction: Tracing Jamaican Musical Legacies and Cultural Legends *1*
DONNA P. HOPE

1. "I Was Born Here": Glocalizing Reggae Music in Belarus *13*
   KLAUS NÄUMANN

2. Tommy Lee as "Uncle Demon": Contemporary Cultural Hybridity in Jamaican Dancehall *45*
   ROBIN CLARKE

3. The Development of Reggae Music in Mexico: A Periodization of Its Adoption and Adaptation *66*
   CHRISTIAN EUGENIO LÓPEZ-NEGRETE MIRANDA

4. Peter Tosh, Social Protest and Jamaican Curse Words *93*
   RACQUEL BERNARD

5. A Kartel of Sin? Messianic Desires and Vybz *126*
   ANNA KASAFI PERKINS

Contributors *149*

ACKNOWLEDGEMENTS

Edited volumes are always a reflection of significant collaborative efforts across multiple borders. My sincere thanks to those who continue to support the thrust to make essays such as these available for consumption by a wide audience of researchers, students and other individuals whose cravings for more lines of text on Jamaican popular music remain unsatiated. The entire staff and faculty of the Institute of Caribbean Studies and the Reggae Studies Unit, colleagues in the Faculty of Humanities and Education, and the wider Mona campus of the University of the West Indies are recognized in this work as key facilitators for the 2015 staging of the International Reggae Conference at which these essays were first presented.

A great deal of respect goes out to the team at the University of the West Indies Press, headed first by Linda Speth and then by Joseph Powell, for their unswerving support and professional attention during this process. To our unnamed reviewers, thank you for your incisive and helpful comments towards the refining of this project. I also wish to personally thank all the contributors herein for their patience, their timely responses and their intellectual contribution to this volume.

In the final analysis, I owe a personal debt of gratitude to my family, including Claudia "Yvonne" Reid, Trevor Reid and Bertland Hope, and to my friends and colleagues Lloyd Waller and Livingston White. The unwavering support of my team at the Mona campus of the University of the West Indies, including Shamar Lester, Tanya Francis, Georgette McGlashen, Trojean Burrell, Hugh Douse, Robin Clarke, Ray Hitchins, Nicole Plummer and Fabian Thomas, has been priceless. Fabian Barracks and Bradson Longsworth also provided key support for the conference staging from which this collection emerged.

ACKNOWLEDGEMENTS

There are never enough words to underscore the multiple networks that converge around the publication of a volume, suffice it to say that those whose names may be omitted from these pages are acknowledged in the breach as ongoing contributors to my research and scholarship and to my academic and personal well-being.

INTRODUCTION

TRACING JAMAICAN MUSICAL LEGACIES AND CULTURAL LEGENDS

DONNA P. HOPE

Who owns reggae? Is reggae Jamaican? Is there an indigenous reggae that supersedes all other forms? Is the term *reggae* synonymous with all forms of Jamaican popular music? This edited collection on representations of Jamaican popular music, musical icons and their glocalizing into diverse spaces is oriented around an era where these controversial questions form part of the national debate in Jamaica and its diaspora about the reach, ownership and exploitation of its popular music forms.

In the contemporary era, the term *reggae* has come to stand in the international imagination as a synonym for "Jamaican popular music" in all its diverse forms and multifaceted glory. And in Jamaica, the birthplace of reggae, this term remains a conflicted categorization. Indeed, many in Jamaica identify reggae as one genre of Jamaican popular music and highlight the same along the formal developmental continuum of the country's music as the fourth national form of music (notwithstanding the presence/development of other secondary forms). Indeed, in Jamaica, as intra-generational and political debates around the value and validity of local music forms ebb and flow in the post-millennial era, reggae is also often identified as the only truly valuable form of Jamaican popular music that has spanned the globe, continuing to make musical inroads across language and geographical barriers. Yet, on the linear continuum of Jamaican popular music forms, it is mento, ska, rocksteady, reggae and dancehall in that order that are highlighted as the primary Jamaican musical forms spanning the 1950s to the present.

What is also noteworthy is that dancehall is the longest dominant form of Jamaican popular music to date. If it is timetabled, as many often do, from its ascendancy in 1980 (also identified as the decline of "good" music and the "bad" turn to dancehall by some), then, to date, dancehall has held sway in Jamaica for almost four decades.

Nonetheless, the ongoing social and cultural debates around "good" versus "bad" music in Jamaica continues to colour the musical landscape. Indeed, during Reggae Month 2016, a caller to my then radio talk show (96Degrees, aired on NewsTalk93FM in Jamaica) was upset that dancehall was getting airplay during "Reggae" Month. "Dancehall must ease off," he insisted. "Ah reggae time now." He was unmoved by my attempts to explain that, according to the organizers, the selection of the name "reggae" for a month to recognize the contribution of Jamaican popular music in all its forms was based on the international perception of Jamaican music as "reggae". "Why them never name it Jamaican Popular Music Month?" he asked. Representatives of the Jamaica Reggae Industry Association, which now spearheads the Reggae Month activities in concert with support from the state and other private sector sponsors, have made many attempts to explain why the month was labelled as such at the outset in 2009 and why their association uses the term *reggae* as a part of its name, even while claiming to represent all categories of Jamaican popular music. Nonetheless, this conflict over appropriate naming and usage of the term *reggae* remains an ongoing debate in Jamaica.

Reggae is an internationally recognized musical genre that is indigenous to Jamaica. Reggae is Jamaica. Reggae is recognized as inextricably linked to Jamaican identity. But even so, reggae is not the sum total of all forms of music that have emanated from the Jamaican people and made their way outwards, via diverse channels, into the hearts and minds of non-Jamaicans across the world. Ska, Jamaica's first internationalized music form, and contemporary dancehall both enjoy significant support and continue to be replicated in various forms across the world. This too is part of the journey of Jamaican popular music. However, at this juncture, this work acknowledges the cultural conflation of reggae and Jamaican identity in the local and international imagination as undisputable. Indeed, the Global/International Reggae Conference, hosted at the Mona campus of the University of the West

TRACING JAMAICAN MUSICAL LEGACIES AND CULTURAL LEGENDS

Indies since 2008, underscores this conflation and signifies the importance of the term *reggae* as a beacon that ignites ideas around all forms of Jamaican popular music in glocal spaces.[1] The variety of conference offerings in its panels, papers, seminars, films and other manifestations over the years recognizes the local/national and global/international forms of Jamaican popular music. The stories that are often narrated around Jamaican music, particularly in the global arena, continue to identify in the same way as stories about reggae and the people of reggae. They are ReggaeStories.

As we advance towards the end of the second decade of the post-millennial era, riding the waves of reggae music and culture, infused by the mega-successes of the Marley brand and the business of Marley, Jamaican popular music seems in clear danger of stagnation. Dancehall music and culture, birthed in the crucible of Kingston's inner cities at the beginning of the 1980s, seem to have held onto the forefront of musical imagination and youthful creation in Jamaica for far too long. This fact notwithstanding, there are renewed celebratory moments and musical output around what has been dubbed a "reggae revival".[2] These are highlighted in what I identify as the second wave[3] of post-millennial Rastafari-inspired reggae artistes like Protoje, Chronixx, Kabaka Pyramid, Jesse Royal, Iba Mahr, Jah 9, Keznamdi and others since 2010. They continue to inflame the popular notion that reggae nostalgia – a yearning for the sociopolitical climate of the late 1960s and 1970s – and a focus on the successes of reggae's emperor, Bob Marley, translate into a revival of this genre and a return, in essence, to the "good old days" of pure reggae. Yet, I assert that one does not "return" to the organic creation of a musical form that is based on dated metaphors harking back to an era that is out of sync with the challenges of the present day. One moves forward and new forms emerge naturally out of new ways of being. Thus, the reggae revival project and its modern-day musical ambassadors must utilize contemporary themes and symbols, even as they broker their market thrust on the success of Jamaica's powerful reggae brand. But, as one reflects on the power of the brand that is reggae and its critical connections to Jamaican identity and the organicism of Rastafari livity, it is undeniable that new artistes from a variety of racial, social and geographical locations races will tread the reggae pathways, locally and glocally, wherever Jamaican popular music holds sway.

There are many narratives about the forms of Jamaican popular music, and the ReggaeStory of Jamaica's most famous musical ambassador, the great Robert Nesta Marley, is dominant among them. Larger in death than he was in life, Marley looms across the body politic of Jamaican popular music, issuing an almost siren song, calling forth renewed waves of claimants to the reggae throne. Many of these would-be inheritors of Marley's cultural legacy pay homage to rituals, symbols and lyrics that have long lost their sting in this post-millennial era, but which find significant traction in the nostalgic yearnings of many reggae fans for the golden era of the past. Nonetheless, one has only to glance at their hands or across their desks to confirm that today's revolution is waged more deliberately across social media platforms (such as Twitter, Facebook, Instagram, YouTube, Snapchat and WhatsApp) that swallow all in their path like some New World black hole. This is contemporary youth culture, and it is within and through these and other digital, internet portals that the narratives of life in music make their most significant headway in today's mobile networks.

Jamaica's ReggaeStories are encapsulated in its popular musical genres like reggae, ska, dancehall and the new, upbeat electronic wave of Jamaican popular music that is yet to take its form and claim its name. These stories are continually transformed through the new digital pathways by which they are disseminated in cyberspace. These transformations have already announced their arrival: see, for example, the contestations over "stolen" dancehall dance forms in Justin Bieber's video for "Sorry" and the Rihanna-fed tropical house debate among others.[4]

In the meantime, the interrogation of Jamaican popular music, what I identify as ReggaeStories and their multiple manifestations across glocal spaces, continues. As such, the chapters in this collection reflect the efforts of a diverse community from a range of places and individuals who have spent hours enjoying the beats and engaging with Jamaican popular music and its multifaceted themes. These are stories of the reach and span of Jamaican music and of the resonating beats that come through sound systems and from reggae singers and dancehall deejays. These are sonic movements that shatter linguistic barriers and touch the souls of people united by desires that take flight on the wings of Jamaican popular music.

Lines of Text: ReggaeStories

The five critical essays in this volume together present an interconnected set of reflections around my concept of ReggaeStories and their resonance with local/glocal identities.

German ethnomusicologist Klaus Näumann shifts the curtain aside and provides critical material about the meanings that have been made of reggae and its stories in the Soviet Union. In his chapter "'I Was Born Here': Glocalizing Reggae Music in Belarus", Näumann utilizes both secondary and empirical sources and his own linguistic agility to open the reggae music scene in Belarus, a former Soviet republic, for exploration by those who may have been limited by language or geography from so doing. Näumann explores a glocalized series of interconnected activities that draw directly from Jamaican forms and expressions, but which ostensibly remain firmly rooted in their locale, claiming strong cultural ties to Belarus: "I was born here." This claim for Belarusian natal origin, while having clear antecedents in Jamaica's reggae music genre, is a critical component of Näumann's chapter. He highlights the role that local actors play in the adoption and adaptation of cultural and musical forms as a part of the movement of these forms outward and into new locales and imaginations that are marked by different racial, social, political and cultural themes.

While markedly different from the traditional sociological/anthropological or cultural studies approaches to discussions about Jamaican popular music, Näumann's ethnomusicological approach provides important material about the musical styles and lyrics that are part of the Belarusian reggae music scene. More importantly, this chapter is the first exploration into the reggae scene in a post-Soviet society that has been made available to an anglophone audience. As such, it is an invaluable component of the narrations of ReggaeStories and their glocal movements. The convergence of political movements, government policies and language restrictions are identified by Näumann as key facets in the unique development of Belarusian reggae, a genre that clearly owes its genesis to the Jamaican form but remains ostensibly Belarusian.

In Jamaica, dancehall's modern-day narratives remain locked in controversy while underpinned by the culture of celebrity that is inherent in contemporary musical production. Cultural studies researcher Robin Clarke presents an inward/outward examination of the contemporary dancehall scene in his chapter "Tommy Lee as 'Uncle Demon': Contemporary Cultural Hybridity in Jamaican Dancehall". Clarke journeys inside dancehall's post-millennial debates and argues for the development of a hybridized subgenre of Gothic dancehall, brokered on glocal themes and epitomized most clearly in the Uncle Demon figure that heralded Tommy Lee Sparta's rise to dancehall dominance in 2012–2013. For Clarke, Tommy Lee Sparta as Uncle Demon deliberately represented himself as a controversial anti-Christian figure to generate controversy that he used to propel himself to the upper echelons of dancehall music and culture. In short, Tommy Lee Sparta engineered a "buss",[5] utilizing local and global means similar to those harnessed by his incarcerated mentor Vybz Kartel.

Dancehall's long-debated fashion, style, posing and nihilism were renewed with Tommy Lee's post-millennial aesthetic codes and body modification choices (including piercings and tattoos) that continue to clash with the moral and ethical values from traditional Jamaican society. Here, traditional Jamaican society continues to be projected as conservative and Christian (fundamentalist) and, as such, its reflections on the "negative" nature of dancehall and its exemplars[6] ignore obvious moments of cross-fertilization with film tropes that have remained interlocked with Jamaican popular music and culture for decades. Certainly 007, Al Capone, Lee Van Cleef and Josey Wales are not indigenous Jamaican tropes, yet these feature prominently in narratives and self-imagined titles of popular Jamaican songs and artistes from an earlier era, including ska, rocksteady and early dancehall.

Clarke's interrogation of Tommy Lee as a glocal dancehall hybrid expands the debate by recognizing the historical connections between Tommy Lee's "Uncle Demon" moniker and earlier manifestations of Afro-Jamaican rituals, beliefs and customs. He simultaneously links the foregoing to modern tropes, including the Euro-American goth/ic aesthetic in popular culture, with manifestations in the popular *Twilight* film trilogy that was immensely popular in Jamaica. Here, Tommy Lee exemplifies the ongoing clash between the local and global and the hybrid manifestations of the same in Jamaican popular music – in this instance, dancehall music and culture – and thus provides a crucial site for the necessary interrogation of the renewed manifestations of Jamaican life and identity.

The enduring play across geographical and linguistic soundscapes as a part of this glocal movement of Jamaica's popular music is brought into stark relief when Christian Eugenio López-Negrete Miranda opens another important pathway through language and geographical barriers to share his insight in his chapter "The Development of Reggae Music in Mexico". López-Negrete Miranda employs a set of textual mechanisms that are at once intriguing and informative. He draws on his multifaceted experience as a Mexican man, a Rastafari, a fan and researcher of reggae and dancehall music and culture, a lecturer, and an individual with a keen interest in Jamaica and Jamaican identity. This multifaceted placement is his most vital tool in his comprehensive and accessible overview of six key periods (from 1965 to present) in the development of reggae and Jamaican popular music forms on the Mexican scene.

López-Negrete Miranda's seminal work in this collection is a critical component of my ongoing project to share unexplored arenas with those in the English-speaking world, and in Jamaica, about the span and influence of Jamaican popular music. He locates the geographical region identified as the Mexican Caribbean as an important contributor to the adoption of the music of Jamaica in a predominantly Spanish-speaking and Catholic context. In so doing, he also considers the necessary connection between reggae music and the cultural and religious platform of Rastafari as it developed on the Mexican scene. López-Negrete Miranda's discussion also briefly explores the development of a Mexican dancehall scene as a complementary musical genre to reggae and provides essential information about key players, events and activities that energize the forms of dancehall culture in Mexico. These include the popular dancehall dance scene, which has made significant inroads globally. López-Negrete Miranda proposes a unique periodization of the development of reggae music in Mexico that provides the reader with an appreciation of the interconnectedness of what are in fact disparate historical moments in Mexican cultural history. As he notes, this periodization is a useful methodological tool for understanding the development of reggae music in Mexico, while simultaneously demonstrating the existence of a stream of Mexico-made music that has had a great influence on Jamaican popular music since 1965. Throughout this chapter, López-Negrete Miranda skilfully highlights the transformation of Jamaican popular music through syncretization with local Mexican culture, and the resulting Mexican reggae (and dancehall) scene, as emblematic of the adaptation that characterizes the glocalizing of Jamaican popular music.

The glocal conversations continue in Racquel Bernard's chapter "Peter Tosh, Social Protest and Jamaican Curse Words". Bernard deconstructs the person and artistry of Peter Tosh as a black radical prophet and a reggae revolutionary who uses word/sound/power in his attack on the status quo. Her exploration of Tosh's response to anti-black rhetoric and systems is framed within the context of Rastafari ideology as liberation theology. Consequently, she positions Tosh as a black Rasta who confronts white bias and deploys both music and language in his attack against the "shitsem". Bernard's work in this chapter adds significantly to the dearth of scholarship on, and critical analyses of, Tosh the man, the artiste and the radical black philosopher. She simultaneously advances a treatise on his musicianship and cultural leadership as they relate to race, protest and social memory.

Tosh's militant and unapologetic stance against state domination is epitomized in his use of Jamaican expletives as lyrical ammunition. Bernard delves into this conflicted interplay between Eurocentric and Afrocentric notions of identity and status in what is seen as "appropriate" (read as English) and "inappropriate" (read as Jamaican Creole or Patois/Patwa) language. Bernard reminds us that Tosh's use of profanity cannot be separated from his concern for social change as his subversion engages with the real consequences of inequality. In weaving disparate pieces together in this textual tapestry, Bernard positions Tosh in a glocal context characterized by global race matters, local Jamaican class biases and Rastafari's incendiary glocal worldview where his subversive/taboo speech acts resonate.

As Jamaica's musical soundscapes continue their inward stretch and outward reach, dancehall music and culture's stars and superstars surge inward and outward in their quest for fans, popularity and resources. Anna Kasafi Perkins's chapter "A Kartel of Sin? Messianic Desires and Vybz" extends the debates around the body of work on Jamaican popular music and its iconic figures. An academic and theologian, Perkins undertakes a unique analysis of Nicholas Alexander's "Season of Fear", a poem incorporating theological and popular imagery. "Season of Fear" is simultaneously oriented around the Lenten season (which is observed in Jamaica) and around the fall of dancehall's dark star and popular artiste Vybz Kartel. She excavates Christian and popular themes from this poem to demonstrate Alexander's poetic imagery of the meanings around the Kartel phenomenon at the time of his trial and conviction for murder in 2014.

Social and cultural leadership are also significant themes at work in the body of the Kartel phenomena. As such, Perkins explores the desire for a paternal leader that emanates from members of the Jamaican populace. In historicizing paternal leadership as a vital component of the postcolonial Jamaican/Caribbean political landscape, Perkins highlights the underlying desires of many citizens (especially those from the working classes) for a messiah, noting that this messianic leader historically hailed from the formal political sector. However, as Perkins argues, in the face of the failure of politicians to adequately address pressing issues of resource allocation among its citizens, other actors have been elevated from below, as in the case of Vybz Kartel (the World Boss) from popular culture. Kartel's rise and his subsequent fall is juxtaposed against the unwavering adulation of his fans that extends beyond his sentencing, and this adulation underscores Perkins's concern for the texture of messianic leadership.

All together, the chapters in this volume epitomize the glocal interplay of meanings and imagination that continues to colour the representations of Jamaica's ReggaeStories as they are deployed across geographical and linguistic barriers. The collection evokes a conversation with Jamaican popular music forms and icons spanning decades, through Rastafari reggae's incendiary and militant politics, its forays beyond geographical borders into a transformed reggae, and Rastafari and dancehall scenes in the Mexican Caribbean. It highlights the identity negotiations at work in reggae's adaptation within post-Soviet Belarus and showcases the modern-day hybrids at work in goth/ic dancehall's interchange with Euro-American tropes. It also examines contemporary manifestations of leadership from below as a component of the ongoing debates around the popular Kartel phenomenon.

The discussions herein are brokered on biographic narration, cultural studies analysis, ethnomusicological interrogation, literary and theological interpretation, and celebrity culture and its posturing. This volume bridges the outmigration of Jamaica's popular music across "salt water" and language barriers and the return home to sun-kissed shores in an ongoing and neverending ReggaeStory of the lives and imaginations of multiple actors in multiple glocalities.

Notes

1. The Global/International Reggae Conference is the brainchild of retired University of the West Indies professor Carolyn Cooper. Since its inaugural staging in 2008, it has been hosted under the auspices of the Institute of Caribbean Studies and the Reggae Studies Unit at the Mona campus of the University of the West Indies as the Global or International Reggae Conference. The term *reggae* is used in this instance to mean all forms of Jamaican popular music in the local and glocal spheres. Consequently, the conference provides opportunities for a range of Jamaican popular music stakeholders, local and international, including researchers, academics, journalists, practitioners and students, to network and engage in panel discussions, seminars, and film and musical presentations around all genres of Jamaican popular music.
2. Dutty Bookman (Gavin Hutchinson), a Jamaican resident in Washington, DC, and self-declared revolutionary and author of the 2011 memoir *Tried and True: Revelations of a Rebellious Youth*, has been credited for popularizing the term *reggae revival* at his book launch. As a movement, the reggae revival is defined on its website (http://reggae-revival.com/the-revival) as being centred on positivity in thoughts, words actions and beliefs. It communicates messages of love and unity through music and is a reflection of the feelings and culture of the current generation, and it notes that one aim of the music is to raise consciousness among the youth and foster a spirit of active involvement in one's own environment. Central to the movement is its claim for an inception among the people rather than a "top down" imposition by those in positions of power within creative and social industries. Key members of this reggae revival movement include artistes Protoje, Chronixx, Iba Mahr, Jesse Royal, Jah9, Keznamdi, Kelissa, Exile di Brave and Dre Island; groups like Nomaddz, Raging Fyah and Pentateuch; deejays like DJ YaadCore; and cultural creators like Dutty Bookman himself.
3. See my discussion on the first wave of this return to Rastafari and reggae at the turn of the new millennium in my article "I Came to Take My Place: Contemporary Discourses of Rastafari in Jamaican Dancehall" (*Revista Brasileira Do Caribe* 9, no. 18 [2009]: 401–23). In it I identify the artistes then associated with

the first wave of this movement, including Natty King, Mr Perfect, Gyptian, Ghandi, Fantan Mojah, Bascom X, I-Wayne and Turbulance. The fact that these artistes were mainly located within the dancehall proved problematic for arguments that attempted to support a return to reggae's earlier themes from its "golden age". This first wave eventually faded with many of these artistes enjoying little visibility on the contemporary music scene. My subsequent discussion on what I identify as the second wave (also self-styled as the reggae revival) of this movement also engaged with this debate and forms the substance of my presentation "New Name? Conceptualizing the Second Wave of Post-Millennial Rastafari Renaissance/Reggae Revival in Jamaican Popular Music" at the the Rastafari Studies Conference and General Assembly, University of the West Indies, Mona, Jamaica, 13–16 August 2013.

4. The debate around the escalating appropriation of both the musical sounds and dance styles, and the corresponding dearth of credit given to the genre's contribution, is exemplified in Justin Bieber's mega-hit "Sorry" in 2015, which utilized a skeletal dancehall beat over a pop sound, complete with choreographed dancehall-style dancing for his video. The choreographer for the video faced significant backlash on social media from Jamaican dancehall dancers and others who felt cheated by not being named as originators of or contributors to the dance styles shown in the video. The debate also escalated with references to Rihanna's January 2016 release of "Work" as tropical house. As noted in Harley Brown's useful piece in *Spin Magazine* online (27 January 2016), "'tropical house' is dance music with fewer than 120 beats per minute, which means you can sort of loosely bop your body around to it — ideally, poolside or on a beach somewhere — without throwing yourself into the faster-paced, harder-edged fray of house music, techno, and EDM. Its easy melodies are constructed almost entirely from synthesized pan flutes, marimbas, and 'Can You Feel the Love Tonight'-lite pianos." Popular Jamaican artiste Sean Paul, in an interview with Hannah Ellis-Petersen of the *Guardian* online (5 September 2016), is outspoken about the new generation of artists who have appropriated the sound of Jamaican dancehall without acknowledging its roots stating: "It is a sore point when people like Drake or Bieber or other artists come and do dancehall-orientated music but don't credit where dancehall came from and they don't necessarily understand it."

5. *Buss* is a Jamaican creole term meaning "to burst out" or get a break into the musical space. It is used in Jamaican popular music discussions, especially dancehall, to suggest the explosive arrival of an artiste to the attention of fans, the media and the wider public. This arrival is usually achieved by committing a controversial act on- or offstage or singing a particularly controversial song

that is guaranteed to generate intense media and social discussion, thereby resulting in widespread publicity, which usually leads to real rewards such as bookings for popular dancehall events or being signed by a producer. However, getting a "buss" does not always translate into long-term economic rewards or consistent fame/notoriety. Many who "buss" end up being "one-hit wonders" who eventually disappear from the scene.

6. For example, in December 2016, an intense social debate arose around the 2017 issue of the local *Yellow Pages* directory cover. As a part of the company's focus on Jamaican popular music, all three covers of the *Yellow Pages* sported art by Lennox Coke showcasing scenes from Jamaican music. The volume, showcasing a dated dancehall scene reminiscent of the late 1980s into the 1990s, came under fire from the Jamaica Coalition for a Healthy Society (religious lobby group) and its associated entities. The scantily clad women, who appeared to be dancing with men in a typical dancehall street scene, were seen as challenging in terms of the conduct being displayed, and the coalition raised concerns about what values "young people" were being exposed to. As noted by Wayne West, chairman of the coalition in a *Gleaner* article (1 December 2016), "We didn't think that scene, which was sort of a dancehall scene, was ideal. It wasn't the best thing that could have been done for the Yellow Pages – something which is so widely distributed and which is supposed to be the product of a company that should be seeking to elevate rather than to encourage behaviour that is not necessarily ideal."

Global Directories, the local entity that produces the *Yellow Pages* directories in hardcopy and online, purportedly issued an alternative copy with a more palatable rendition for those who desired it. However, the ensuing heated debate raged on in traditional and social media for several weeks.

CHAPTER 1

"I WAS BORN HERE"
Glocalizing Reggae Music in Belarus

KLAUS NÄUMANN

Bands performing **Western-orientated popular** music that incorporated sub- and youth cultures have existed in the Soviet Union since the late 1940s. This phenomenon started with jazz in its multiple variations and continued on through late 1950s rock 'n' roll and in 1960s beat music (or big beat), with the Beatles being the most important band. From the 1970s, the spectrum widened once more and included different varieties of rock, new wave, punk and eventually reggae music, which will be highlighted in this chapter through the example of Belarus. The authorities of the different Soviet republics always viewed the Western-style bands and their fan bases with suspicion. They sometimes tolerated these bands, but authorities more often marginalized, prohibited and even persecuted them. An exception was a small number of state bands which were supported by the governments. It was not until Gorbachev's glasnost and perestroika policies (starting in 1985) that the restrictions on unofficial popular music bands were eased. In the period of decline and the subsequent dissolution of the Soviet Union in 1992, these new developments eventually led to the diverse scenes of popular music as they exist today in the former Soviet republics and they continue to remain mostly unexplored (Ryback 1990; Troitsky 1987).

Reggae Music in the Soviet and Post-Soviet Union

Where and when the first bands of the Soviet Union with some link to reggae were founded may likely only be clarified through the greatest effort.

However, this is not the primary concern of this chapter. What is of concern here is that in the late 1980s – still during the Soviet period – Jim Riordan (1988, 563) indicated in a scientific paper that influences of reggae music were to be found among groups in the Soviet Union. Unfortunately, Riordan refrained from delving any further into the subject and providing more details.[1] Steinholt (2003, 93, 103) in turn, however, expounded on how the Russian band Aquarium, in their recordings on their album *Taboo* (cassette 1982, CD 1994), incorporated reggae influences (in addition to punk and ska) into their music.[2] In the late 1980s the Russian journalist and author Artemy Troitsky (1987, 50) came to a similar conclusion, stating that Aquarium's music at the beginning of the 1980s was limited exclusively to reggae in an acoustic variant (that is, largely unamplified). Beyond this, Troitsky points to a music festival in Tbilisi (Georgia) in 1980 as being one of the most important events of the past concerning the development of rock music in the Soviet Union. During this festival – which actually was a music competition – the Estonian rock and funk group Magnetic Band performed a reggae song for which they were announced as the winners of the entire competition (Troitsky 1987, 50). However, despite Magnetic Band's success at the festival, Troitsky (108) asserts that the first "real reggae band" of the Soviet Union (even smoking ganja in Moscow's Red Square) was the Russian band Misty in Roots. This assertion notwithstanding, Troitsky's revelation that a Baltic group (Magnetic Band from Estonia) was among the early pioneers of reggae music in the Soviet Union is still noteworthy and not to be dismissed. This fact correlates in toto with the existing body of knowledge about popular music during the Soviet era. According to the level of knowledge, a disproportionate amount of band activity occurred in the Baltic states (especially in Estonia and Latvia) in comparison to other regions of the Soviet Union during the communist era (Ryback 1990; Troitsky 1987). With regard to the importance of reggae in the Baltics, internet sources on this desideratum suggest that since the late 1970s, particularly in Estonia, reggae influences were incorporated into the repertoire of some groups.[3]

Beyond this rather sporadic use of some reggae elements (for example, playing chords with electric guitar or keyboard on the beats 2 and 4 at a moderate pace) since 1987, the existence of Ensemble Komitet Okhrany Tepla from Kaliningrad is particularly noteworthy. This band is the first case (as

"I WAS BORN HERE": GLOCALIZING REGGAE MUSIC IN BELARUS

far as I know) where explicit self-positioning in reggae is evident – insofar as their first recordings (1987) are titled *Rastamen* (Растаманы). In the song "Summer Will Be Soon" ("Скоро Лето") on that LP, for example, the phrase "Hey, where are you Rastamen?" ("Хэй, где вы растоманы?") is striking.

Also attributable to these early forms with apparent concessions to reggae is the group Jah Division, for which the singer of the band, Gerbert Morales, claims that Jah Division was not merely the first reggae band of Russia, but the founder of the entire Russian reggae scene. Furthermore, based on the following quotation, another factor that may have been crucial to the development of a reggae scene in Russia becomes visible – namely, punk music: "In part, reggae [in Russia] emerged from the punk music. Elements of reggae music were used by well-known musicians like [Alexander] Barykin or [Boris] Grebenshchikov. Rasta Reggae Roots movement began with Jah Division in the 1990s. We (Jah Division), if I may say so, are the founders of Russia's reggae" (Anonymous 2010). The question of which band was actually the first one in the Soviet Union to utilize reggae in one way or another notwithstanding, it can be stated that since the late 1980s, a growing openness towards music with Caribbean flair in general, and music with Jamaican influences (reggae, ska and so on) in particular, has evolved. This seems to be yet another factor contributing to different reggae scenes in the various former states of the Soviet Union becoming more visible since the new millennium and with the growth of the internet.[4] In today's Russia, there exists a large number of bands (including Alai Oli, Kaya Warriors, Akljusija) who pick up and reinterpret reggae in its ever-changing varieties (roots reggae, dancehall, dub, ragga and so on).[5]

Along with Russia (the largest and most populous republic of the former Soviet Union) today, there are reggae scenes in many other former Soviet republics. These scenes include bands that are either partly or fully linked to this genre.[6] With regards to the Ukraine (primarily in the area of the city of Kharkiv), Adriana Helbig (2011, 315, 320, 324) asserts that students coming from different African countries (Uganda, Kenya, Nigeria) have had a certain impact. In addition to establishing numerous hip-hop scenes, these students have spurred an increase of activity in the area of reggae.[7] Concerning most of the other countries of the former Soviet Union: at this point in time, one is only able to get an impression of the myriad activities via the World Wide

Web.[8] In addition to sound systems, festivals, concerts and the like, reggae or bands with an affinity for reggae exist assuredly in Georgia (for example, Reggaeon), Lithuania (for example, Ministry of Echology, Shidlas), Latvia (for example, Riga Reggae, Strikis, Hospitāļu iela), Estonia (for example, Number Ö, Loudi, Bombillaz), Armenia (for example, Reincarnation), and Azerbaijan (for example, Jin), and, concordantly, in Belarus, which moves us now into the main focus of this chapter. Before moving on, however, it should quickly be noted that the groups in the above-mentioned countries incorporate their local languages into the lyrics of their songs.

The Historical and Political Situation around Reggae in Belarus

Belarus went through a complex history before becoming a sovereign state in 1991. Today, the country is regarded as the last "dictatorship of Europe" or "the last communist bastion". The regions that belong to the Belarusian territory now have (since the fourteenth century) been divided (in varying shapes and sizes) among the great powers of Russia, Poland and the Grand Duchy of Lithuania. Significant parts of the current collective memory of Belarus are the German occupation connected to atrocities against the population (1941–1944), the Chernobyl reactor accident of 1986 that caused an environmental catastrophe in the southern regions of Belarus, and the finding of mass graves of victims of the NKVD (the police and secret police) of the Stalin era in a forest near Kurpaty (close to the capital, Minsk) in 1988. Due to this history, and especially due to the decades of Sovietization and Russification, a singularly Belarusian identity could only weakly unfold. Additionally, the Belarusian language, a separate East Slavic language, remained marginalized for long periods of history, thus causing a further dilution of Belarusian identity. However, surprisingly, in 1990 – immediately before the collapse of the Soviet Union and the Belarusian sovereignty (1991) – the Belarusian language was declared as the only official state language. However, so few people were able to speak the language at that time (due to the endurance of Russification) that in 1995 the Russian language was declared an additional official language. Since then, as was the case for much of the country's history, the Belarusian language again became marginalized. Today, the Russian language dominates unambiguously in everyday life. The

"I WAS BORN HERE": GLOCALIZING REGGAE MUSIC IN BELARUS

FIGURE 1.1. Map of Belarus

Belarusian language, in contrast, is present only in certain spheres, such as some theatres and museums, in certain academic circles, as inscriptions on public buildings, and in numerous concerts of (especially) rock bands.[9] Due to these specific historical, social and language developments, in modern-day Belarus there exist bands who interpret reggae both in Belarusian and in Russian.

Musical Characteristics of Reggae

In order to expound on the characteristics of reggae in both Belarusian and in Russian, at least a brief discussion concerning the musical characteristics of "Jamaican reggae" itself is required. Such a discussion is complicated, however, by the fact that, today, diverse types and interpretations of reggae coexist. Since its beginnings in the 1960s, the genre has been constantly evolving – a phenomenon that can be exemplified by the musical endeavours of personalities such as Bob Marley.[10] Thus, more pragmatic definitions of reggae must be undertaken. These are briefly outlined here using the following two classifications: a *conservative* definition (= roots reggae) and a *modernist* definition. It must be added that we are by no means dealing with clear, distinguishable phenomena. Instead, the boundaries are fluid.

First, concerning a conservative definition of reggae, one can list musical traits that largely overlap with many pre-existing brief definitions, introductions to the genre, instrumental playing instructions and, probably also, with many European listeners' primary associations.[11] European listeners often associate reggae with the music as it has been played since 1972, particularly by the Wailers. This music was a combination of Jamaican and English influences as far as production and mixing were concerned. It was a popularized variant of reggae for the international market that has, over time, been generally referred to as "roots reggae". Roots reggae consisted of two important aspects: namely, the distinct associations with Rastafarianism and the central hero-figure of Bob Marley (1973–1981) (cf. Wickström 2011, 155 ff.).[12]

Delving more deeply within the framework of a conservative definition, one trait essential for this music was an instrumentation consisting of electric guitar, bass guitar, keyboards (at times), small brass sections (trumpet, trombone, saxophone), drums, percussion (conga, bongo, tambourines, shakers and so on) and a singer who sings either in a Jamaican patois or at least in English with a patois accent. The singers generally neither have nor use a great range of tones, nor do they sing falsetto or use vibrato. The German musicologist Peter Wicke (1998, col. 133) stresses the incantatory repetitions of the central text statements that occur in the consistently repeated musical passages.

"I WAS BORN HERE": GLOCALIZING REGGAE MUSIC IN BELARUS

The pace of reggae songs is within a frame of about 120 to 155 beats per minute (measured by the crotchets).[13] And so another essential characteristic of this music is the riddim. Riddim is the approach where, using the electric bass (with boosted low frequencies), ostinato figures (by which certain songs can be directly identified) are played. This musical observation leads into yet another trait essential to this genre, and that is the way in which the electric guitar is played. It can be done by playing skank or bang (which means playing staccato chords in off beats [2 and 4, or the quavers in between the beats]), by the accompanying or supplementing of the riddim (often muted), or by playing additional monophonic fill-ins. Sometimes the skank or bang playing-style is also carried out using the keyboards. A common accentuation (for example, using rim shots) is played on the third beat with the snare drum.

Reggae songs are exclusively in straight metres (usually 4/4 or 2/2 bars). However, the rhythm can be in either a swing-style or straight. Concerning the harmonic structure, songs consist of major and minor chords – occasionally with sevenths (major 7, minor 7), and also a dominant seventh chord. It can be completely objectively stated that reggae is not and shall not be virtuoso music. Rather, "feeling" dominates. As well, in terms of the formal structure, the songs usually do not contain strongly contrasting interludes, long solo parts, intros or outros.

As previously mentioned, apart from musical characteristics, roots reggae is strongly connected to Rastafarianism – with its (here assumed as known) inherent values systems (which are often reflected in song lyrics), followers' physical appearance (for example, dreadlocks) and in the exhibition of a particular mode of behaviour (specific language, smoking ganja).

The modernist definition of what constitutes reggae could be briefly stated as follows: all of the listed essential traits of the conservative definition of reggae (with respect to roots reggae) can vary. Musical influences and instruments from any musical idiom or genre may appear. Within the modernist definition, reggae is merely a word that, over time and across geographic locations, has continually had its meaning expanded and changed with regard to its musical and extra-musical components.[14] This has become particularly significant since the 1980s and especially since the dawn of the new millennium when various hybrid forms and styles emerged. New terms like "dancehall reggae", "dub reggae", "raga" or "ragamuffin", and "reggaeton" emerged to give expression to these changes in the genre. Reflecting on all of these terms and their more-or-less existing inherent musical traits would quickly get out of hand. Instead, from this point forward, the focus will be directed onto the interpretation of reggae in Belarus.

Belarusian Reggae in Belarus

Since the 1960s in the Soviet Union, there have existed state bands (so-called VIAs – Vokalno instrumentalny ansambl) that were officially allowed to perform popular music in a compromised form that encompassed (among other things) the image, the appearance of the musicians and the repertoire.[15] Therefore, in the Soviet Republic of Belarus, some state bands (Pesniary, Verasy, Sjabry) also were formed that, in contrast to other states of the Soviet Union, used the Belarusian language in the lyrics of their songs. However, in the music of these government-sponsored ensembles, influences from reggae did not occur: during this period (the 1960s), reggae was just in its early stages in Jamaica and, had it been known, the inclusion of reggae in the repertoire of a state band would not have been considered respectable.

Gorbachev's perestroika and glasnost policy (since 1985) led to greater freedoms in Belarus. At that time in Belarus, numerous bands were formed that (similar to the official Belarusian bands) also used the Belarusian language in their lyrics.[16] When Alyaksandr Lukashenka was appointed president, and when, just one year later, the Russian language was declared an additional official language (to the Belarusian), these newly formed bands – as well as the entire Belarusian national movement – found themselves increasingly marginalized. The occurrence of these two historical events meant that Belarusian bands were hardly able to perform in their own country, especially in the urban areas. The only opportunities they had to perform were in smaller clubs away from the larger cities or abroad (Germany, Poland, the Baltics, Russia), where there were no restrictions.[17] This situation remained largely unchanged until recent years.[18]

Concerning the musical style of these groups, we are dealing mainly with rock music and its various subcategories.[19] Explicit reggae bands do not exist in this context, though some bands rather sporadically incorporate reggae or

"I WAS BORN HERE": GLOCALIZING REGGAE MUSIC IN BELARUS

reggae elements into some of their songs.[20] The (undoubtedly) most famous song with a connection to reggae, which most Belarusians of the younger generations presumably know, is "I Was Born Here" ("Я нарадзіўся тут"). The song originated in 2000 from a project and a sound recording of the same name ("Я нарадзіўся тут"). The music and lyrics were composed by a prominent Belarusian musician, Liavon Volski (of the bands NRM, ZET and Krambambula), likely in cooperation with the also well-known musician Z'micier Vajciushkievich (of the bands WZ Orkiestra and Palac). Both are considered to be musical figureheads from the period of the national awakening in Belarus from the mid- to late 1980s through to 1994 (see Petz et al. [2007]).

The song "I Was Born Here" has many of those characteristics listed in the conservative definition of reggae presented earlier in this chapter.[21] The pace is about 130 beats per minute (measured by the crotchets), the metre is a 4/4 time in swing feeling. In addition to the vocals, the instrumentation consists of electric guitar, electric bass guitar, keyboards and unobtrusive percussion. Brass instruments are absent. The formal structure consists of two parts based on the chord progressions d–d–C–g–d–e–d–d (verse) and a–a–g–g–a–a–d–e (refrain). With the electric bass, a line (one similar to a reggae riddim) is played (see figure 1.2). Despite occasional variations, this bass line is doubled by the electric guitar. Virtuosity does not play a role,

FIGURE 1.2. Riddim-like bass line in the verse of the song "Я нарадзіуся тут" together with the vocal melody in Belarusian language

even though some short guitar solo passages occur (long tones and eighth movements dominate). Uniformity and "feeling" dominate.

What is more is the use of rim shots with the snare drum. This technique, resulting in an accentuation of the third beat, comprises parallels to Jamaican roots-reggae songs. Further, as stated by Peter Wicke (1998, col. 133), the central message or vocal passage is repeated many times – almost in a meditative manner. Also, from the phrasing of the vocals (with occasional crotchet triplets), similarities to roots reggae result in which this rhythmic figure is commonly used. The accentuation of the second and fourth beat in skank or bang manner is carried out with the keyboard. The crucial component that differs distinctly from Jamaican reggae is the language – namely, Belarusian. The central phrase "I Was Born Here" ("Я нарадзіуся тут") underscores the Belarusian origin. The lyrics deal with everyday life in today's Belarus, with all its related deprivations. Nevertheless, the message of the lyrics is a clear commitment to the country in which the people (in this case the musicians) were born:

> Я нарадзіўся тут
> У краіне пад шэрым небам.
> Я нарадзіўся тут
> У краіне бульбы, калгасаў і чорнага хлеба.
> Я нарадзіўся тут
> У краіне прапіскі і скручаных кранаў.
> Я нарадзіўся тут
> У краіне сотняў парушаных храмаў.
>
> *Refrain*
> Радзільня, дзіцячы садок,
> Школа ды інстытут.
> Я нарадзіўся тут,
> І я буду жыць тут
>
> I was born here
> In a country under a grey sky.
> I was born here
> In the country of the potato, kolkhozes and black bread.
> I was born here
> In a country of citizen registration and twisted cranes.

"I WAS BORN HERE": GLOCALIZING REGGAE MUSIC IN BELARUS

I was born here
In a country of hundreds of damaged churches.

Refrain
Maternity ward, kindergarten,
School and college
I was born here
And I will live here.

The significance of sociopolitical or even heretical aspects of the music and in the lyrics written by the artists who emerged from the national movement of the 1980s is further made clear in a song by Alyaksandr Pamidorou (Аляксандр Памідораў). Pamidorou is primarily a rock musician (vocals, guitar) who writes lyrics in the Belarusian language. Since the increased marginalization of Belarusian-language rock music (1994), Pamidorou, like his contemporaries, has only been able to give concerts under severe restrictions. Therefore, he now mainly performs as a soloist (vocals, guitar) and no longer in a band line-up. On 18 September 2012, I was able to attend one of his concerts and, afterwards, conduct an interview with him on the premises of an unofficial opposition group located in a building in the city of Minsk. As a part of this concert, political prisoners were commemorated. In addition to the photos of the arrested individuals being displayed, the now-banned Belarusian flag, along with the emblem – the so-called Pagonia – were also posted throughout the room (see figure 1.3).

One of the songs Pamidorou performed during this evening was entitled "Dawaj ustawaj" ("Давай ўставай") which means in English, "Get Up Stand Up". And, indeed, this was a Belarusian-language solo version (vocals, guitar) of the classic reggae tune by Bob Marley and Peter Tosh (1973):

Мы стомленыя ад вашых ізбаў і яркі
і яркі выстаўленыя ад лжывыя прапаганды.
Гэй прапаведнік, ці ты разумееш,
што ўсіх нас не задушыш, ты ўсіх нас не заб'еш.

Refrain
Давай ўставай за свае правы,
давай ўставай, не кідай барацьбы!

FIGURE 1.3. Aljaksandr Pamidorou on the premises of an opposition-group building in Minsk, performing the song "Dawaj ustawaj". *Left*: The Pagonia; *middle*: pictures of imprisoned opposition activists; *right*: the now banned Belarusian flag.

> We are tired of your (palatial) houses
> and we are exposed to a highly mendacious propaganda.
> Hey preacher, don't you (really) understand,
> that you can not strangle all of us, that you can not kill us all.
>
> *Refrain*
> Let's stand up for your rights,
> Let's get up, don't give up the fight!

It is obvious that, due to the solo performance (vocals, guitar), sufficient parameters for reflecting on either a conservative or modernist definition as they might apply to this song do not exist. The reference to reggae in this case is constituted by the song itself and by the semantics of the lyrics. As in the original English version, the message of the Belarusian lyrics is a combative call, with a Christian background, addressed to citizens who are oppressed by a dictator (or a "Babylon-like" system), put forth as a catalyst for escaping the oppression. The parallels between the original song lyrics and the prevailing situation in Belarus since 1994 are obvious.

Belarusian-speaking reggae is a peripheral phenomenon. Bands or solo artists use reggae only now and then in order to (likely) generate a broader musical stylistic diversity and (likely) because the music is particularly well-suited to lyrics containing revolutionary potential. An explicit and exclusive assignment to reggae (including Rastafarianism) is not the intention of these groups and artists.

Russian-Language Reggae in Belarus

When I conducted ethnomusicological field research on urban music in Minsk in 2012 for the second time, I (rather accidentally) came across the existence of a small scene of younger bands who had dedicated themselves explicitly to reggae. The club scene in Minsk is limited to a few small and medium-sized locations. Within these clubs, concerts (predominantly of Belarusian bands and partially of solo artists) take place.[22] The music performed at these places can be defined as rock, folk and bards-music, or, more broadly, popular music.[23] In addition to the Pirate Club and TNT, Club Graffiti is one of the most important locations for the scene and concerts take place there almost every day. On 2 September 2012, the band Botanic Project gave a concert at Club Graffiti (see figure 1.4). It was noteworthy that, during the performance, the majority of the audience – who, visually, did not suggest any discernible affiliations to reggae music (for example, dreadlocks, t-shirts with Bob Marley or a hemp leaf) – knew most of the lyrics and were loudly singing along. It seemed that the band was of above-average popularity, at least in the capital of Minsk.

The members of the band Botanic Project (which was founded in 2006) come from Molodechno (Молодечно), a town approximately seventy kilometres north-west of Minsk. The band line-up consists of two singers with musicians playing the instruments (percussion, electric bass, electric guitar/acoustic guitar, keyboards, saxophone/flute and drums). In addition to Belarus (where only limited opportunities for performances exist), the band has played concerts across Eastern Europe, in Poland, Kazakhstan, Siberia

FIGURE 1.4. The reggae band Botanic Project during a concert at Club Graffiti

and in the bigger reggae festivals of Moscow and St Petersburg.²⁴ In addition, the group has already received several awards for their musical achievements (for example, for the compact disc Делай своё дело). To date, the group has released four compact discs (Нормалия 2008, ОМ 2010, Реанимация 2012, Делай своё дело 2014). Botanic Project categorizes themselves as a "Belarusian reggae group" ("белорусской регги-группы") and describe their style as "reggae/dub" as well as "reggae/hip-hop/ragga-jungle/funk".²⁵ How the band discovered reggae is revealed through a member's statement: "The choice of style depended on the music that we were listening to in the beginning of the 2000s. We loved reggae music with all our hearts, and it is this love that, in the end, we were gathering together. . . . We try to convey to people that reggae is primarily a protest, (a) depth and (a) spiritual search" ("Kesh Man", pers. comm., 26 August 2015).²⁶

The music of Botanic Project is mainly based on roots reggae – that is, the conservative definition of reggae. This also suggests the instruments that are used. However, the fact that two singers take part in the band results in both an alternating and a simultaneous (sometimes also two-part) singing of the vocals. For a vast number of songs, the skank playing on the beats 2 and 4 is used. The way of playing the bass is often, but not always, close to a riddim. The harmonies are often (as is usual for roots reggae) simply structured and even refer concretely to well-known reggae pieces such as "No Woman, No Cry" (for example, "Цирк" 2010).

In his book *Rock in Russia* (1989, 24), Artemy Troitsky points out that the high estimation of the Beatles in Russia is based on the fact that they used beautiful, catchy melodies in their songs. Whether this is the case or not should be left undecided here, as well as the answer to the question of whether Troitsky was also referring, by making such a statement, to other East Slavic countries such as Belarus. For, indeed, several roots reggae-oriented songs by Botanic Project comprise melodies that are similar to folk or pop songs ("Voin" 2014, "Почему" 2012, "На легке" 2010).

Moreover, what is remarkable is that in some of the group's songs that are relatively close to roots reggae, instruments that are atypical to reggae are used. Some examples include the violin ("Почему" 2012); the accordion, which is even used for playing skank chords ("Останься" 2012); and some acoustic string instruments that are difficult to identify by ear (possibly a domra in "Делай Своё Дело" 2014). Furthermore, the band integrates into their roots reggae–related songs some scratching ("В танце" 2010) and some heavily distorted rock guitar sounds – at times either as a solo or as accompaniment ("Ночь в тишине" 2014). Significantly, modernist tendencies, concerning the vocals, occur in some of the songs. In these cases, the singing style is close to ragga or raggamuffin, inasmuch as only a few tones within a narrow range are used, and the rhythmic aspect dominates ("Do Not Worry, Mama" 2014, "Большие глаза" 2010). In addition, it is remarkable that chords often finish ringing with a kind of retardation effect (such as quaver triplets), and due to the use of reverb and delay effects, certain instruments (and especially the vocals) sound "back, far to the rear".

Modernist tendencies can sometimes also be found within the harmonic framework where modulations in neighbouring tonalities occur ("Rastaman Live Up" 2014), or where even jazz-like chord progressions can be found ("Девять дней и ночей" 2014). Jazz-oriented lines and solos are also played at times with the saxophone ("Едкий дым" 2014).

When compared to roots reggae, various songs by Botanic Project can be said to be arranged more "extravagantly", with elements such as intros, interludes, the dynamics with a particularly heightened mood and tempo ("Война" 2012, "Сам не свой" 2012, "G-meditation" 2012). Therefore, some of the pieces rather remind one of reggae pop songs in the vein of the Police, UB40 or Men at Work (for example, "Rastaman Live Up" 2014).

In a few of their songs, the band rejects all references to reggae (both *conservative* and *modernist* definitions). What results are pieces that partially comprise bossa influences ("Мухоморный вальс" 2014) or are pop ballads ("Почему" 2012), some pieces are rock songs ("Воздушный шар" 2012, "Сон" 2010) while others have a disco flair ("Om" 2010, "Бабло" 2010), and some of the band's pieces are reminiscent of so-called world music ("Дарья" 2012) or contain rudimentary Indian influences ("Кришна" 2010). This eclectic approach by the band can produce motley mixes of styles ranging from reggae (a bit), to rock, to pop, to folk and jazz ("Время подумать" 2012, "Кем был кем стал" 2012, "Снайпер" 2012).

The semantics of the lyrics by Botanic Project are fairly versatile and ambiguous, which makes a precise ascription to certain themes difficult in some cases. In all, the band explores themes of personal welfare (including, at times, songs with an autobiographical bent to them) and of asking philosophical questions (about the meaning of life, enlightenment or salvation),[27] but their lyrics also question war and the existence of soldiers ("Voin" 2014, "Война" 2012). Quite often, religion plays a role. The five world religions (Hinduism, Judaism, Islam, Buddhism and Christianity) are put on equal footing in the band's work, in which the name *Jah* – strongly associated with Rastafarianism – is most frequently mentioned ("Только Jah" 2008).[28]

Furthermore, reggae and/or Rastafarianism-related aspects are concretely referred to in connection with the situation in Belarus. In the lyrics of the song "Do Your Thing" ("Делай Своё Дело" 2014), for example, the band stresses that it devotes itself entirely to reggae, while at the same time making it clear that their intention is not to be devout as though they were in Jamaica but, rather, to adapt reggae to Belarus:

> Лигалайз марихуана, время быть самим собой
> I n I Алтайский край, мы на Ямайку не хотим
> У нас здесь такой риддим – за штакет сел до седин
> Сплифы крутим из green-карты, мы не трусы-эмигранты
>
> Legalize marijuana, the time to be yourself
> I 'n' I, we belong to the Altai region, we don't want to go to Jamaica.

"I WAS BORN HERE": GLOCALIZING REGGAE MUSIC IN BELARUS

> We do have a Riddim here²⁹ – for smoking a joint here, you will sit (in jail) until you get grey hair.
> We turn the green card into a splif (because) we are not cowardly emigrants.

The following passage from the song "I'm Not Myself" ("Сам не свой" 2012) is worth examining. What is unmistakable here, again, is that despite accentuating some similarities ("rude boys") with the Jamaican country of origin, a distinct profile of reggae in Belarus is maintained as its own theme:²⁷

> Вот они, вот они, вот они rude boys этой системы
> Прячутся с пипетками31 за шторами под вой сирены
> Botanic project, Аддис Абеба не латино, не Jamaican-ganjamana-african-аборигена.
>
> Here they are, here they are, here they are, the rude boys of this system
> Together with good looking girls they hide behind the curtains from the howling sirens
> Botanic Project, Addis Abeba are no Latinos, are no Jamaican ganja-crazy inhabitants of African origin.

(While this last phrase may seem pejorative, it might be interpreted rather as underlining the Belarusian origin of the band.)

Furthermore, in their lyrics, Botanic Project sometimes overlays the Babylon system onto the specific situation in Belarus ("Ночь в тишине" 2014).³² When taking other lyrics into account, one can imagine the social objections to or even the marginalization of Rastas in Belarus. One of the few songs written in English (at least partially) – "Do Not Worry, Mama" (2014) – illustrates how the protagonist discovered Rastafarianism and reggae and, thereafter, how he has to allay his mother's apprehensions about this: "I'm not a rocker, I'm not a rapper, I'm a Rastaman. Don't worry mom, if your son is a Rasta" ("Я не рокер, я не рэппер – я растаман. Don't worry mama if your son a Rasta").³³

The lyrics of the song "Vampire" ("Вампиры" 2012) deal with the lines of demarcation that exist between the Belarusian majority society on the one side and reggae fans and Rastafarians, with a different set of values (honesty, freedom and vitality) on the other. A passage where this becomes evident is the following line from the song: "We build a wall between us [and them] of honesty and faith" ("Построим между нами стену из честности и веры"). Sometimes, but not in an overly expressive manner, drugs (ganja) and their use are discussed in the lyrics ("Большие глаза" 2008).

The focus of the band's lyrics also, at times, revolves around the lack of (political, cultural and individual) freedom in Belarus. In "Freedom" ("Swobodo" 2014), for example, note the following passage: "Freedom, that's not the whisper in the kitchen, my friend. Freedom is the clear, loud sound" ("Свобода это не шёпот на кухне, мой друг, Свобода это громкий и отчётливый звук").

No less noteworthy are those texts that do not contain any (obvious) reference to reggae or Rastafarianism, but instead are focused exclusively on life in Belarus today. In "Don't Go" ("Не выходи" 2008), grey, everyday life and work in Belarus are discussed. In the lyrics of the song "Dough" ("Бабло" 2008), low Belarusian wages and incomes are criticized because they prevent the savouring of the pleasures of life (even at least once). Critical remarks about Belarusian politics or personalities are made subliminally, for the most part. Only occasionally is direct criticism or even the spoofing of politicians put forth.[34]

Besides Botanic Project, there exist other Belarusian bands that display some affinity for reggae (for example, the bands Растение мудрости and Тёплые вещи). One of the most prominent of these is, undoubtedly, Addis Abeba (Аддис Абеба), whose name, at first glance, already seems to suggest some association with the genre.[35] The standing of the ensemble in Belarus (and, more broadly, in Eastern Europe) is comparable to that of Botanic Project. Addis Abeba has, like Botanic Project, appeared at major Eastern European reggae festivals (Moscow, St Petersburg) and received, through an internet voting process, an award for "the best Russian (!) Reggae Album".[36] Up to now, the band has released four compact discs (Аддис Абеба 2006, *Live* 2007, Шифроваться 2009, Механизм 2012). The members of the group, which was founded in 2002, are from Minsk. They call themselves Rastas, they call the band a "reggae band from Belarus" and they categorize their music as being of the "reggae, dub, jazz, hip-hop, ragga muffin, ragga core" genres. Furthermore, they emphasize the inclusion of different influences (from jazz to hardcore) in their music.[37]

"I WAS BORN HERE": GLOCALIZING REGGAE MUSIC IN BELARUS

This self-description is quite accurate. On the one hand, their repertoire is often based on roots reggae ("Дымом уходили" 2009), but, in most cases, their music involves elements that qualify it as needing to be classified as unconventional or modernistic. This means (among other things) the inclusion of flute sounds (via keyboard) ("Музыка счастья" 2006), simultaneous use of fiddle and melodica (probably played with a keyboard) ("Емеля" 2009), use of the accordion ("Косяк" 2012), steelpan sounds (also probably played with a keyboard) ("Раггамафин" 2007) and roots reggae's uncommon use of the guitar (acoustic guitar solos, guitar-picking passages, heavily distorted electric guitar sounds) ("Собака" 2012).

Addis Abeba often use various delay, reverb and other alienation effects, especially for the vocals ("Косяк" 2012). As is also the case with Botanic Project, chords that finish ringing with a kind of retardation effect can be heard quite often. In some songs (such as "Гриб-трип" 2009), the array of different types of sounds, effects and noises (faded-in real and mimicked animal sounds) generates a kind of "psychedelic" mood. What is remarkable, in terms of the singing, is that the vocalist alternates between roots reggae–oriented singing and an imitation of raggamuffin (see figure 1.5), and this not only within one song but even within certain verses ("Глупцы" 2009). Furthermore, the singer sometimes even integrates throat singing ("Менты" 2006). Regarding the harmonic structure, the band often uses simple progressions similar to roots reggae. But quite often, similar to Botanic Project, modulations in neighbouring keys occur (as in "Глупцы" 2009 and "Дзеці" 2009).

FIGURE 1.5. Fragment of a vocal line from the song "Raggamafin" ("Раггамафин" 2007; tempo: approx. 129 bpm). Principally, the song is based on roots reggae, but (according to the title) the vocals are close to raggamuffin.

As well, in keeping within the modernist tendencies, consideration should be given to the fact that the group, immediately after a roots-reggae part, plays passages that are similar to punk music (for example, "Шифроваться" 2009). This is particularly evident in the title "The Dog" ("Собака" 2012), which appears to move along the continuum of rock (in the drum grooves), raggamuffin (vocals), heavy metal (guitar) and jazz (piano solo). This modernist, or almost progressive, approach becomes even more evident in the title "I Wash My Hands" ("Умываю руки" 2012), in which, despite all the alienations and escapades (delay effects, saxophone solos, drum-playing style, initial absence of the bass), the reference to reggae nevertheless exits (skank on 2 and 4). That reggae, at least in Belarus, may also include virtuoso elements becomes apparent in longer, solo passages ("Емеля" 2009) and in instrumental interludes ("Эники-беники" 2012).

However, many of the group's songs are far from a conservative definition of reggae. Often in these cases, the only rest reference to reggae is the skank-playing on 2 and 4 (usually with the guitar). The song "Love" ("Любовь" 2006) is an example of this: the style of playing the bass does not have anything in common with a riddim, the use of the drum set is completely dispensed with and even the skank-playing is no longer used. Instead, the 2 and 4 are accentuated in between the playing patterns of the organ (or rather, a synthesizer with organ sounds). In the concrete case of "Love" ("Любовь" 2006), it is only the vocals that make reference to roots reggae, not least due to the fact that, on occasion, the word *reggae* appears in the text.

Some of the songs of Addis Abeba are modelled on ska. That basically means that these songs have a faster pace with inherent semiquavers rhythm and the constant playing of syncopes on the quavers in between the beats ("Птичий грипп" 2007, "Армия Jah" 2007, "Пиу-пиу-пиу" 2009). However, many of the group's songs do not show any association to either reggae or ska. Instead, these songs are reminiscent of Latin rock ("Ноты-минуты" 2006), punk ("Чернобыль" 2006), swing ("Вася" 2006), folk ("Каханая" 2006), funk ("Море" 2009) or rock ("Moonlight" 2007). Some songs also comprise a certain (presumably intended) affinity to so-called Balkan music (Емеля" 2009). Other songs, even the most well-known of the group ("Детка" 2009), are inspired by bossa nova ("Сука-весна" 2012).[38] The fact that the group likes to play with dialectic and antagonism makes itself apparent in the

"I WAS BORN HERE": GLOCALIZING REGGAE MUSIC IN BELARUS

track "Rastaman" ("Растаман" 2012), which, musically, is a clear reference to Cuban music but by no means to reggae (of any kind).

The lyrics of Addis Abeba often deal with general aspects of life, such as God, the earth, the universe, love, happiness, summer and sun. Sometimes there are descriptions of landscapes (often of the beach and sea), partially (likely) containing autobiographical elements. It is noticeable that the lyrics of later albums are less concrete and more philosophical or metaphorical. However, in the majority of the texts, it becomes immediately clear to which kind of music and genre they are connected. They have located themselves within the context of roots reggae and thus also within the Rastafarian faith. Frequently, one can find in the lyrics phrases that are about King Solomon, the Queen of Sheba, Jah, His Imperial Majesty, Babylon (with respect to the Babylon system), as well as dreadlocks, Rastafarians and, of course, the central figure of Bob Marley.

For reasons of space here, only a brief example will be added: in the lyrics of the song "Thanks" ("Спасибо" 2006), the following passage in English appears: "Thank you, Jah, for your love. Thank Jah for reggae."[39] Furthermore, in the lyrics, drugs in various forms (such as ganja, spliff, hashish) are discussed. The text of the song "Short Life" ("Жизнь коротка" 2006), focuses on a drug addict who infects himself with the HIV virus through injecting (presumably) heroin. Among other references, the following statement appears (probably from the perspective of the protagonist): "There is nothing better than putting a dose into the vein" ("Ничего прекрасней нет, чем пустить по вене дозу"). In the song "Mushroom Trip" ("Гриб-трип" 2009), a hallucionogenic trip after taking magic mushrooms is described.

But even exclusively Belarus-specific topics serve as themes. Discussed are, among several of their themes, corruption, the police state[40] and the avian influenza ("Птичий грипп" 2006). The lyrics of "Chernobyl" ("Чернобыль" 2006) deal with the Soviet trauma of 1986 that affected the Belarusian region near the city of Gomel:

> Один мой товарищ в Чернобыле жил,
> но ядерный взрыв этот город поразил.
> Поразил он еще и ученых зоологов,
> а также акушерок и гинекологов.

> A friend of mine was living in Chernobyl,
> but a nuclear explosion damaged this city.
> It also hit scholarly zoologists yet,
> and above that midwives and gynecologists.

Although the lyrics of Addis Abeba are almost entirely written in Russian, a (very) few exceptions of lyrics written in the Belarusian language ("Дзеці" 2009, "Каханне" 2007) can be found in the repertoire.

Altogether, the lyrics of both groups (Botanic Project and Addis Abeba) do not show any homophobic tendencies – as is the case for so-called Jamaican battyman tunes or murder music (by Buju Banton, Beenie Man, Sizzla and Elephant Man, for example). The terms *battyman tunes* or *murder music* refer to a subgenre of Jamaican reggae and dancehall songs. In these lyrics, which are often difficult to understand for native English speakers, homosexual men are denigrated and there are even calls for violence (sometimes fatal) against them. The term comes from Jamaican Creole/patois where the word *batty* is used to refer to the bottom or anus. In some Western countries, musicians who sing these songs are not allowed to perform. While the term *battyman tune* is explicitly Jamaican, the term *murder music* was brought into play by the British activist Peter Tatchell in the 1990s. Murder music, in the broadest sense, refers to any music that calls for violence (among other things, against homosexuals), but in the narrower sense it is again associated with certain Jamaican musicians. Russian-speaking reggae in Belarus tends to equate with ideals such as cosmopolitanism, tolerance, peace and love – in the sense of the hippie movement – even though clear statements against exploitation and oppression appear.

With regards to the development of this relatively young and small reggae scene in Belarus, the following presumption arises: since the time (from 1994 to the present) when prominent Belarusian-singing bands were being increasingly marginalized and were hardly permitted to appear in public, a void was created that offered young bands a space in which to establish themselves. Characteristic of these bands of the younger generation is that they often (likely for political reasons or a lack of knowledge) relinquish the use of the Belarusian language and mainly sing in Russian instead. At the same time, by using the Russian language, they have access to a wider audience – namely, the former states of the Soviet Union where the Russian language is still spoken as a lingua franca (or is at least understood). Although there are only a small number of reggae bands among these Belarusian groups, these reggae bands are an integral part of a transnational Eastern European reggae scene.

Glocalization

The development of reggae, starting from its original location in Jamaica and spreading out to many corners of the world today (including Belarus), is remarkable. A music that emerged from ska and rocksteady (two musical genres that also originated from a highly complex conglomerate of native and foreign styles)[41] during the Jamaican post-independence era in the 1960s was transformed again under foreign (British) influences in the 1970s into a worldwide music style that people were listening to and playing. This music was taken up and reinterpreted by predominantly non-Jamaicans of different continents (Africa, Europe, America, Australia) while it continually changed further in Jamaica. Newer developments in reggae (dancehall reggae, raggamuffin, reggaeton and so on) later emerged – again from the centre (Jamaica), spreading out and further sparking more global changes in listening and playing preferences. A little later than in Western Europe, these processes extended to Eastern Europe where, after initially sporadic revisitings of reggae occurred, finally a transnational Eastern European reggae scene emerged – not least due to the growing importance of the internet. As in other countries of the world, reggae (in all its variations) was adapted to specific circumstances and repurposed, and specific national languages were incorporated– even those of some of the smaller language communities (from Estonian to Georgian).

Phenomena such as these have been treated in ethnomusicological discourse since the 1990s under the heading of "globalization" – a highly ambiguous term, often used in a pejorative sense. This globalization, however, is not a unilateral flow from the "West to the rest" (Stokes 2004, 48) – a trend which ultimately leads to a cultural homogenization, or the "cultural grey-out" – because local factors make themselves apparent as a result of "the realities" (cf. Nettl 1983). The Indian anthropologist Arjun Appadurai (1990, 295), who became a leading figure in this discourse, stated that "as rapidly as forces from various metropolises are brought into new societies they tend to become indigenized in one or other way: this is true of music". In order to take the factor of "the local" within the context of "the global" into account, sociologist Roland Robertson (1995) (inspired by a Japanese art neologism) introduced the term *glocalization*. The core idea of glocalization may be clarified through the following statement by sociologist George Ritzer (2003, 193): "Glocalization can be defined as the interpenetration of the global and the local, resulting in unique outcomes in different geographic areas." This definition, refined by sociologists and anthropologists, was revisited by ethnomusicologists (for example, Slobin 1992; Turino 2003).[42] However, the ways in which (in at least some cases) these theories within the context of ethnomusicology were treated are criticized, for example, by Ingrid Monson (1999, 32):

> Not much emphasis has been placed on musical sound itself. This is not surprising since theoretical perspectives on the global and the local have been dominated by social scientists, philosophers, and literary theorists. Ethnomusicologists have attempted to squeeze their concerns into the vocabularies of these interdisciplinary discussions, but have not often made a case for what musical processes themselves might have to offer these larger theories of social and cultural interpretation.

Monson's criticism can be partially justified, despite the fact that it dates back almost twenty years. However, the theory of hyper-culturalism by Byung-Chul Han (2005) is, in my estimation, for the issue at-hand, of particular relevance. Han's assertion further refines the theory of glocalization by taking into account the factor of the internet. In his theory, Han assumes an utter dissolution of cultures, beginning on the internet and ensuing into the real world, which creates a hyper-cultural sound space. In this space, diverse sounds are thrust in juxtaposition to one another without any distance between them (Han 2005, 13). According to Han, in this hyperspace, the various forms of culture (including music) are delocalized and can (at least theoretically) be accessed from any location, demystified ("entaurarisiert") (42) and reinterpreted in the respective local conditions. Of great significance in Han's theory is that the ostensibly different cultures by no means need to enter into a direct dialogue (as is the premise of the theories of multi- and interculturalism). Despite this, as Han states, these processes create a sustainable change for participants, as well as for the old and newly emerging forms of culture (here, music). Monotony is in no way the result of these processes, but rather a local or regional differentiation "beyond 'beautiful' and 'ugly'" (67).

This theory by Han seems to partially comprise idealistic notions (of a better world in spite of the internet). Moreover, it is based on the premise that, in fact, all over the world, and for all people, the internet is more or less always available (which is not the case).[43] Still, many thoughts important for this topic of discussion are to be found in his theory. Belarusian bands utilize an extraneous genre (reggae music in all its forms) and reinterpret it for their own specific (social, political, historical) situations; however, the phenomenon is not based on real contact with Jamaican reggae musicians or any migratory movements. Also, it is not a kind of Westernization (in the pejorative sense) imposed on a so-called threshold country from the outside. As well, economics-based marketing strategies (inside or outside the country) play, at best, a subordinate role (in view of the fact that a system of profit-oriented music management in Belarus hardly exists). The main actors are, in fact, the musicians (along with their fanbases) who extract from a "hyper-cultural sound space" (primarily the internet, as well as compact discs, vinyl albums, television, radio) music ranging from roots reggae to ragamuffin – along with their associated values (Rastafarianism) – dechronologize it, and then glocalize it with local characterizations.

The claim of authenticity is not raised by the groups (neither by the one singing in Belarusian nor by the one singing in Russian); rather, they emphasize the particularities of Belarus in their music. These local components become apparent in the lyrics – that is, the language that is used and the semantics. Less simplistic is the matter of the musical characteristics that often cannot be unambiguously attributed to processes of glocalization (exception: the inclusion of the instruments of the respective culture). Yet, at the same time, for the supporters of this scene, the most pleasing effect comes in the experiences of listening and viewing – which are both familiar (language, semantics, musicians) and, from a Belarusian perspective, "exotic" (reggae).

Notes

Unless otherwise indicated, all translations in this chapter are the author's own.

1. Performances by Western bands were certainly conducive to the popularity of reggae music, as were concerts of the group UB40 (1980) in the Soviet Union. But regardless of such important events, citizens in the Warsaw Pact who were interested in popular music and its developments in the West were often well informed (see Ryback 1990; Troitsky 1987).
2. Cf. also Wickström (2010, n.p.).
3. See, for example https://www.mixcloud.com/sovietgroove/soviet-reggae-since-1977/ (accessed 11 August 2015). The recordings to be found there are labelled with the phrase "Soviet reggae artefacts, mainly from Republic of Estonia /1977-1986/".
4. Concerning specifically Belarus, see Survilla (2002, 80). A pioneer of this has probably been Santana, whose songs have been covered by Russian bands since the 1970s (see Ryback 1990, 153).
5. Furthermore, in Russia there are some reggae labels, recording studios, internet channels, websites, homepages and blogs. Moreover, reggae and dancehall parties as well as festivals take place and, once, an attempt was made to establish a reggae contest for bands and producers ("Reggae Got Talent 2009"). See Anonymous (2010).
6. To quote here at least one example of an Eastern European country, namely Poland, that did not belong to the Soviet Union, Patton (2012, 428) mentions, but does not describe in detail, that the phenomenon "Reggae in Poland" already existed during the times of martial law (1981–1983). Regardless of the development since that time, today a distinct reggae scene exists in Poland, even containing bands in Upper Silesia, who perform reggae music in the Polish Silesian dialect. Furthermore, during field research about the music of the Germans in the former West and East Prussia in 2006, I accidently discovered and attended an annual reggae festival in the Masurian Ostróda (Osterode).
7. In this respect, Helbig (2011, 324) refers to the band AfroRasta. Moreover, her essay makes (implicitly) clear that the African students are often exposed to racist insults.
8. See also the freely accessible film on different internet platforms: *Almaty by Bus: A Reggae Documentary from China to Kazakhstan*.
9. I have explained this in detail (including the sources) elsewhere (Näumann 2014, 163–67).
10. The musical development (combined with the intensifying effect of the religious devotion to the Rastafarian faith) becomes easily apparent in the most

"I WAS BORN HERE": GLOCALIZING REGGAE MUSIC IN BELARUS

important exponent, Bob Marley, when comparing his early recordings (such as the ska-attributable "Simmer Down" 1964) to later recordings (such as "Could You Be Loved" 1980). This is also the case for many other Jamaican artists whose music changed during their careers and therefore is assigned to different genres. Similary, the music of Derrick Morgan (born 1940) is sometimes associated with ska and sometimes with reggae. His title "Tougher Than Tough" (1966), in turn, is referred to as the beginning of rocksteady. This also applies to Desmond Dekker (1941–2006), whose music is partially attributed to reggae and partly to ska.

11. In this regard, for example, René Wynands argues in his book on reggae (2000, 90) that there is a strong contrast between the Jamaican reggae audience, who prefer "rougher" variants and the non-Jamaican public, who favour "smooth, shallow, melodious, harmonious, straightforward" music. However, it is limited to what extent these words can explain a fairly complex situation. Nevertheless, the references made to different audience tastes (in and outside of Jamaica) are noteworthy and would be worth exploring in more detail.

12. It should be mentioned that there is, to an extent, a distinction being made between the internationalized form of reggae and roots reggae (see Wickström 2010). However, it would reach beyond the scope of this chapter to describe this matter in more detail.

13. In order to give some examples for the tempo of roots-reggae songs, measured by the crotchets (and not the half notes as it is often done): Bob Marley "Buffalo Soldiers", about 124 beats per minute; Peter Tosh "Bush Doctor", about 136 beats per minute; Dennis Brown "Whip Them Jah", about 139 beats per minute; Gregory Isaacs "Babylon Too Rough", about 144 beats per minute; Johnny Clarke "If You Should Lose Me", about 151 beats per minute.

14. While doing fieldwork about mento music in Jamaica in February 2015, I experienced how the idea of musical characteristics constituting reggae may diverge among researchers, musicians and musicologists. In conversations with passengers about their musical preferences during bus trips, many told me that they primarily listen to reggae music. However, the reggae sound samples that they shared with me (on MP3 players or mobile phones), I would never have associated with reggae before this experience.

15. See Ryback (1990, 106, 150 ff.); Troitsky (1987, 18, 54 ff., passim); Cushman (1995, 77 ff.).

16. This includes, for example, the bands Mroja (formed 1982), Bonda (formed 1984), Sartipo (formed 1988), Ulis (formed 1989), Nejro Dziubel (formed 1989), Ljapis Trubetskoj (formed 1990), Krama (formed 1991), Novaje Nieba (formed 1991) and Palac (formed 1992).

17. See Näumann (2014); Petz et al. ([2007]); Petz (2012); Survilla (2002, 136 ff., and 2003, 197).
18. It needs to be added that after my field research in 2010 and 2012, it was not until 2013 that I was able to see some of those bands live in Belarus for the first time (for example, Krama, Nejro Dziubel, and Ljavon Volski and Pavel Arakelian). In 2013, it seemed that the rigid policy towards those bands had become slightly more relaxed. However, not even the people concerned could explain to me why this was the case.
19. The music of the bands Nejro Dziubel and NRM can be categorized as heavy metal/hard rock, the music of Krama is attributable to blues, whereas the music of Palac and the WZ Orkiestra falls in the category of folk and ethno rock.
20. See, for example, the song "The Best Girl" ("Лучшая девушка") of the band Nejro Dziubel on their LP *stasi* (2007).
21. Liavon Volski (email, 13 August 2015) simply responded to my question of whether this song could be categorized also, in his point of view, as reggae: "Yes, that is Reggae, of course." Quote in the original: "Da, eto reggey, oczewiscie [*sic*]."
22. The concerts of famous international bands take place elsewhere – for example, in the Minsk Concert Hall or the Minsk Arena.
23. Commercial pop music, also called Popsa, is generally excluded from this. See Cushman (1995, 124 ff.).
24. This is, on the one hand, the Reggae Festival Moscow, which took place for the sixth time in 2014, and on the other hand, the slightly younger Piter Reggae Festival, which took place for the second time in 2014.
25. See the various websites of the band: https://www.facebook.com/bpromusic; https://vk.com/botanic_project; https://vk.com/bpromusic.
26. Original quote: "Выбор стиля зависел от музыки которую мы слушали, в начале 2000ых мы полюбили музыку регги всем сердцем и именно эта любовь и собрала в итоге нас вместе. . . . Мы пытаемся донести до людей что регги в первую очередь это протест, глубина и духовный поиск".
27. This is the case for the lyrics of the song "Time to Think" ("Время подумать" 2012).
28. For more song texts where this is the case, see "Едкий дым" (2014), "G-meditation" (2012), "Только Jah" (2008), "Цирк" (2008), "Спираль" (2008), "Едкий дым" (2014), "G-meditation" (2012), "Только Jah" (2008), "Цирк" (2008) and "Спираль" (2008).
29. This could possibly be a ruse, in so far as the word *riddim* in this context can easily be understood (or interpreted) as "regime", and thus would be an expression of political protest.

30. See also the lyrics of the song "Rastamen" ("Растаманы" 2012). The text of the song "The Uncle" ("Дядька" 2012) is (probably) about Bob Marley, even though his name is not explicitly mentioned.
31. The word "Пипетка" is a colloquial term for a young, likeable, good-looking woman.
32. In the mentioned song "Night of Silence" ("Ночь в тишине" 2014), the following statement is noteworthy: "You're always a captive, you're always the loser, chant down the old Babylonian office employee." In the original: "Ты всегда узник, ты всегда лузер, Chant down Babylon офисный планктон."
33. For reference to the alienation towards the parents that evoked a devotion towards rock in the Soviet Union, see also Cushman (1995, 63 ff.).
34. In the song "Big Eyes" ("Большие глаза" 2008), the following statement is noteworthy: "Haile Selaisse I is our imperator. He bothered us, he bothered us, our moustachioed dictator." Original: "Хайле Селассие I наш император, Надоел, надоел нам усатый диктатор." It is quite obvious which Belarusian political leader is meant here.
35. The connection of Rastafarianism to Ethiopia, and therefore also to its capital, Addis Ababa, is assumed to be known here.
36. See http://www.worldareggae.com/artists/addis-abeba-аддис-абеба/ (accessed 10 August 2015).
37. Cf. the various websites belonging to the group: https://www.facebook.com/addis.ababa02, http://addis-abeba.ad.by/kontakty/.
38. In a remix (2012), the song "Baby" ("Детка") even resembles a kind of lounge music in house style.
39. The same is true for the songs "Абиссиния" (2006), "Африка" (2006), "Дымом уходили" (2009), "Армия Jah" (2009), "Эники-беники" (2012), "Растаман" (2012), "Вавилон" (2006).
40. In the first verse of the song "Vasya" ("Вася" 2006), the following passage is noteworthy: "My name is Vasya, hello, I'm a representative of the authorities, I am militiaman, guardian of the law, from the police department of the Central district." In the original: "Меня зовут Вася, здрасьте, Я представитель власти, Я милицыянер, хранитель закона, Из РУВД Центрального района."
41. These developments are described in an essay by Witmer (1987). He outlines that ska, rocksteady and, finally, reggae developed out of American (including African American) and European influences (gospels, minstrels, vaudeville shows, orchestral music, European brass band, military music, blues, jazz, swing, rhythm and blues, rock 'n' roll), Caribbean music (for example, calypso) and indigenous, partly rural Jamaican music (mento, Burru or Rasta drumming).

42. Slobin (1992, 4 ff.) refers directly to Appadurai's (1999) theory of different scapes. Turino (2003, 52 ff.), however, describes these scapes as too abstract (for music), rather distructs the globalization concept and Instead speaks of "cosmopolitan culture".
43. During my fieldwork on mento music in Jamaica (2015), it became obvious that many of my informants who live in rural areas do not have any (even occasional) access to the internet.

References

Anonymous. 2010. "Reggae in Russia: Producer, Artists and More". http://www.house ofreggae.de/news/1823-reggae-russia-producer-artists.html. Accessed 18 August 2015.

Appadurai, Arjun. 1990. "Disjuncture and Difference in the Global Cultural Economy". *Theory Culture Society* 7 (295): 295–310.

———. 1999. "Global Ethnoscapes: Notes and Queries for a Transnational Anthropology". In *Migration, Diasporas, and Transnationalism*, edited by Steven Vertovec and Robin Cohen, 464–83. Cheltenham, UK: Edward Elgar.

Cushman, Thomas. 1995. *Notes from Underground: Rock Music Counterculture in Russia*. Albany: State University of New York Press.

Han, Byung-Chul. 2005. *Hyperkulturalität*. Berlin: Merve Verlag.

Helbig, Adriana. 2011. "'Brains, Means, Lyrical Ammunition': Hip-Hop and Socio-racial Agency among African Students in Kharkiv, Ukraine". *Popular Music* 30 (3): 315–30.

Monson, Ingrid. 1999. "Riffs, Repetition, and Theories of Globalization". *Ethnomusicology* 43 (1): 31–65.

Näumann, Klaus. 2014. "Wie in der urbanen belarussischen Rock- und Popularmusik *Altes neu gedacht* wird". In *"Altes neu gedacht" – Rückgriff auf Traditionelles bei Musikalischen Volkskulturen*, edited by Klaus Näumann and Gisela Probst-Effah, 163–89. Aachen: Shaker-Verlag.

Nettl, Bruno. 1983. "Cultural Grey-Out". In *The Study of Ethnomusicology: Twenty-Nine Issues and Concepts*, 345–54. Urbana: University of Illinois Press.

Patton, Raymond. 2012. "The Communist Culture Industry: The Music Business in 1980s Poland". *Journal of Contemporary History* 47 (2): 427–49.

Petz, Ingo. 2012. "Im Geiste der Freiheit". *Musikforum* 2 (12): 48–50.

Petz, Ingo, et al. [2007]. [Booklet for the CD] *Belarusian Red Book: Music of Belarus*. Deutsch-belarussische Gesellschaft.

Riordan, Jim. 1988. "Soviet Youth: Pioneers of Change". *Soviet Studies* 40 (4): 556–72.

Ritzer, George. 2003. "Rethinking Globalization: Glocalization/Grobalization and Something/Nothing". *Sociological Theory* 21 (3): 193–209.

Robertson, Roland. 1995. "Glocalization: Time-Space and Homogenity-Heterogenity". In *Global Modernities*, edited by Mike Featherston, Scott Lash and Roland Robertson, 25–44. London: Sage Publications.

Ryback, Timothy W. 1990. *Rock around the Bloc*. New York: Oxford University Press.

Slobin, Mark. 1992. "Micromusics of the West: A Comparative Approach". *Ethnomusicology* 36 (1): 1–87.

Steinholt, Yngvar B. 2003. "You Can't Rid a Song of Its Words: Notes on the Hegemony of Lyrics in Russian Rock Songs". *Popular Music* 22 (1): 89–108.

Stokes, Martin. 2004. "Music and the Global Order". *Annual Review of Anthropology* 33:47–72.

Survilla, Maria Paula. 2002. *Of Mermaids and Rock Singers: Placing the Self and Constructing the Nation Through Belarusan Contemporary Music*. Vol. 2 of *Current Research in Ethnomusicology*. New York: Routledge.

———. 2003. "Ordinary Words: Sound, Music, and Meaning in Belarusan-Language Rock Music". In *Global Pop, Local Talk: Language Choice in Popular Music throughout the World*, edited by Harris M. Berger and Michael Thomas Carroll, 187–206. Jackson: University Press of Mississippi.

Troitsky, Artemy. 1987. *Back in the USSR: The True Story of Rock in Russia*. London: Omnibus.

———. 1989. *Rock in Russland. Rock und Subkultur in der UdSSR*. Wien: Hannibal.

Turino, Thomas. 2003. "Are We Global Yet? Globalist Discourse, Cultural Formations and the Study of Zimbabwean Popular Music". *British Journal of Ethnomusicology* 12 (2): 51–79.

Wicke, Peter. 1998. "Reggae". In *MGG Sachteil 8*, edited by Ludwig Finscher, 132–35. Kassel: Bärenreiter Metzler.

Wickström, David-Emil. 2011. *"Okna Otkroi" – "Open the windows!" Transcultural Flows and Identity Politics in the St Petersburg Popular Music Scene*. Stuttgart: Ibidem-Verlag.

———. 2010. "My Reggery: Reggae, Ska and Ska-Punk in St Petersburg". http://norient.com/academic/wickstroem2010/. Accessed 19 August 2015.

Witmer, Robert. 1987. "'Local' and 'Foreign': The Popular Music Culture of Kingston, Jamaica, before Ska, Rock Steady, and Reggae". *Latin American Music Review/ Revista de Música Latinoamericana* 8 (1): 1–25.

Wynands, René. 2000. *Do the Reggae: Reggae von Pocomania bis Reggae und der Mythos Bob Marley*. http://www.oktober.de/reggae/. Accessed 11 August 2015.

Discography

Addis Abbeba. 2006. Аддис Абеба. CD. GEL Record Studio.
———.. 2007. *Live*. CD. GEL Record Studio.
———. 2009. Шифроваться. CD. Самиздат.
———. 2012. Механизм. CD. Самиздат.
Botanic Project. 2008. Нормалия. CD. [unknown].
———. 2010. OM. CD. [unknown].
———. 2012. Реанимация. Самиздат.
———. 2014. Делай своё дело. CD. [unknown].
Various Bands [2007]: *Belarusian Red Book: Music of Belarus*. Ingo Petz et al. Deutsch-belarussische Gesellschaft.

CHAPTER 2

TOMMY LEE AS "UNCLE DEMON"
Contemporary Cultural Hybridity in Jamaican Dancehall

ROBIN CLARKE

This chapter focuses on dancehall artiste Tommy Lee Sparta and his representation as Uncle Demon. It argues that Tommy Lee Sparta represents a discursive move away from traditional discourses of Rastafari and fundamentalist Christianity in postcolonial Jamaica towards a new hybrid. This hybrid is achieved by conflating gothic aesthetics and tropes, Afro-Jamaican religious beliefs, North American *Twilight* popular culture[1] with that of Jamaica popular music culture – that is, dancehall music and culture. The dark, anti-Christian, demonic stylistic cultural identity of Tommy Lee Sparta is rejected and negated in Christendom and other forms of hegemonic discourses of representations about what constitutes good and bad, right and wrong, moral and immoral. Particularly during their respective heydays, all forms of Jamaican popular music, including mento, ska, rocksteady, dub, reggae and dancehall – have been negated in hegemonic discourses that wield the power of institutional authority in Jamaica. These forms of music were, and to some extent are still, considered a part of residual/low/inferior culture. On the other hand, the exported forms from colonial culture – for example, opera and classical music, have been embraced by a neocolonial aristocracy in the country. While many of the former negations may be true of the criticisms of Jamaica popular music, Tommy Lee Sparta is criticized by dancehall artistes themselves (such as Bounty Killer and Ninja Man), who see him as transgressing the preferred culture of dancehall and Jamaica by embracing an entity that has never been embraced in Jamaica or in Jamaican popular music and culture – that is, the devil or demon. Tommy Lee Sparta's defiant stylistic expressions embrace the unforgivable as he, along with contemporary artistes such as Alkaline, discursively move away from traditional aspects of dancehall music and culture that constitute components of the Jamaican identity as a Christian country. Here, Tommy Lee Sparta's persona disturbs the religious conscience of fundamentalist Jamaicans and tampers with the sacred narratives of Judeo-Christianity and its institutional discourses that are part of Jamaica's traditional hegemonic sphere.

For the purpose of this chapter, the manifestation of Tommy Lee as Uncle Demon is specifically examined through his live performances, dark videos, lyrical treatises, sartorial dress-code, (personal) interviews, and his adoption of various tattoos and body markings. In attempting to unpack some of the meta-narratives surrounding the entertainer, I argue that Tommy Lee forms an alliance with Vybz Kartel of the Portmore Empire by relocating to the new hub of dancehall gladiators and deliberately introduces a cultural hybrid that generates controversy. He then utilizes this controversy to propel himself to the upper echelons of dancehall music and culture. This rise to the top tier of dancehall was further facilitated by the physical absence of Vybz Kartel, king and ruler of the Portmore Empire, who remains incarcerated at the time of writing.

Dancehall's Genesis/Genealogy

Dancehall is the musical genre of Jamaican popular music that emerged in the late 1970s into the early 1980s routed/rooted in the sound system culture of the 1950s and the early "toast" or "talk over" style originally done by U Roy, Big Youth and King Tubby among others. Following on the heavily Rastafari-influenced debates in its musical and cultural predecessor reggae, dancehall evolved into a cultural phenomenon that incorporates a self-sustaining subculture that includes fashion, style, attitude, dance moves, lyrical treatises and live performances. Researchers identify the dancehall as a physical as well as a sociopolitical space that speaks chiefly to debates about poverty, violence, sexuality and social justice (see Cooper 1993, 2004; Hope 2006a, 2010, 2011; Stanley-Niaah 2010; Stolzoff 2000).

The genesis of dancehall music and culture represents a watershed moment in the genealogy of Jamaican popular music. This distinct musical form and its accompanying culture came to the fore in the 1980s, a period described as Reaganism and Thatcherism by Stuart Hall (1979) and other cultural analysts (Stanley Niaah 2005), when the new world order moved to neoliberalism or free-market capitalism. These shifts also affected Jamaica's cultural, technological, political and economic life. For example, Jamaicans had lost hope in the *smadditization*[2] of the 1970s and in Michael Manley's democratic socialist policies and the conservative movement of Rastafari as well as the conscious lyrics of reggae. Reggae, dancehall's immediate predecessor, emerged in the 1970s at a time when the festive feeling of ska and rudeboy rocksteady are said to have failed to bring about revolutionary changes in the lives of Jamaica's poor in the post-independence era (Chang and Chen 1998). Arguably, a new set of revolutionaries (such as Burning Spear, Peter Tosh and Bob Marley) came with reggae music, particularly in its roots rock reggae form, significantly influenced by the tenets of Rastafari. Thus, reggae's religious overtones were brokered on Rastafari's interpretation, including the rebranding of a white Jesus with a black one, deification of His Imperial Majesty (HIM), the acknowledgement of a new ancestral heaven in Ethiopia and a new wave of black consciousness that gripped Jamaica in the 1970s (see Hope 2001, 2006a; Stanley Niaah 2010).

At the global level, there was much consternation among world powers, such as the United States and the United Kingdom, and their allies about the spread of communism and its diluted form, socialism. Socialism, embraced by Caribbean states such as Grenada and Jamaica, was supposed to have been one of the planks to help Jamaicans become "smaddy" (someone of worth), manifesting in socio-economic independence. However, coupled with democratic socialism was an agreement with the International Monetary Fund that forced the Jamaican government to adopt draconian financial measures, resulting in the state welfare policies being dramatically cut or completely stopped. This meant that socio-economic independence was not forthcoming as touted and poor Jamaicans were left at the margins of an already impoverished state to fend for themselves. At the end of the 1970s into the early 1980s came reggae's successor, dancehall. The rise of dancehall music and culture is said to have signalled cultural, social and economic shifts from Michael Manley's democratic socialism to Edward

Seaga's North American capitalism (Meeks 1996, 132). Dancehall is also identified by some as a deviant form of music and culture that moved away from the "conscious reggae" era that was wrapped up in African pride, black nationalism and a pan-Africanist ethos. To date, dancehall is described as the ultimate manifestation of Jamaica's move away from Christianity and the "conscious reggae" years.³ At this nexus, the persona of Tommy Lee Sparta, the artiste, can be read as a rejection of the Rastafari/reggae ethos that is arguably more popular overseas than in Jamaica at this historical moment. His current popularity, especially among dancehall fans, attests to this fact.

Tommy Lee Sparta and the Gaza Empire

Tommy Lee's point of entry onto the dancehall stage took place first in Montego Bay in 2008 with the song "Spartan Soldier" and later in Portmore, St Catherine, as a part of Vybz Kartel's⁴ Gaza Empire. Tommy Lee, like dancehall artiste Popcaan, is a protégé⁵ of Vybz Kartel and his Portmore Empire. Tommy Lee, therefore, forms part of a trajectory of controversial figures beginning, for purposes of this chapter, with Bounty Killer,⁶ who could be seen as the grandfather, Bounty's protégé Vybz Kartel being the father and Kartel's protégé Tommy Lee Sparta as the son. Another critical trajectory linked to geography that is not to be missed in the lineage of these artistes is that Bounty Killer hails from Seaview Gardens in Kingston, Vybz Kartel from Portmore in St Catherine, and Tommy Lee from Montego Bay in St James. This geographical lineage is important to the larger debates in the media and within Jamaican popular music: both Tommy Lee Sparta and Vybz Kartel operate outside the original nucleus of dancehall – that is, the inner-cities of Kingston.⁷

While Kingston remains the creative cluster of Jamaican popular music, Vybz Kartel and many of his "offspring" who are associated with Portmore and St James have made a permanent mark on dancehall historiography and geography in Jamaica. In this regard, Vybz Kartel repositioned the zone of authentic production away from Kingston and managed to propel Portmore into musical/lyrical prominence with his use of labels such as Portmore Empire or Gaza Empire. This repositioning of the locus of cultural production of popular music signals a challenge to Kingston as the hub of creation of dancehall gladiators. In the words of Tommy Lee Sparta, "man psycho / Gaza run bout yah" (This man is crazy. Gaza runs the place). Tommy Lee becomes the real-life version of Ivan (played by Jimmy Cliff) in the movie *The Harder They Come,* a poor youth from rural Jamaica who a look a "buss"[8]*inna di dancehall*.[9]

The repositioning of Portmore, St Catherine, as the site for production of dancehall gladiators and its branding by Kartel as Gaza are both critical in the re/creating and re/claiming of musical turf. At the international level, Gaza is a plot of land that simultaneously joins and separates Palestine and Israel in decades of war. Each claims this plot of land as its own. At the local level, a section of Waterford, Portmore, originally called "Borderline", was rebranded "Gaza" when popular roots-theatre actor Keith Shebada Ramsay[10] uttered the infamous line "me deh pan de borderline" [I am on the borderline] in the play *Bashment Granny*. Gaza is symbolic of a territory that must be defended both lyrically and, some would argue, physically, because it has become an empire. It is this plot of land/empire that Tommy Lee must defend (especially in the physical absence but musical presence of the emperor, Vybz Kartel). He reminds listeners/onlookers:

> Me foot plant like a tree root.
> yet still Adijah a me father.
> me come fi rule and me nuh response.
> in case you never known me nah leff the Gaza.

> My foot is planted like the root of a tree
> Yet Adijah [Vybz Kartel] is still my father
> I have come to rule and I do not care
> In case you did not know, I am not leaving the Gaza.

Thus, in adopting the name Sparta both for his own image as well to reflect his connection to the name given to a section of the Flankers community in Montego Bay, St James, Tommy Lee becomes a Spartan, a warrior figure who must fight to maintain his place as heir to the Gaza throne and to stay relevant inna di dancehall. Yet Tommy Lee Sparta's gladiatorial move as a dancehall artiste is not new; his attempt to transcend his ordinary status and become a superhero/warrior figure within the dancehall is similar to what others have done and continue to do in this space. Indeed, warrior figures in dancehall include Bounty Killer (The Warlord), Super Cat (The Wild Apache), Merciless, Assasin, Mad Cobra, Ninja Man and Josey Wales (The Colonel) among others – all hardcore dancehall artistes who lyrically jousted to claim a presence in the upper echelons of the dancehall. Tommy Lee Sparta makes this point:

> I am Uncle Demon and I am proud. . . . Everybody in dancehall play a character; everybody want to be different; you do not want to be nobody else. So you have Beenie Man is a doctor, everyone knows he is not a real doctor; you have Ninja Man who is not a real Ninja, he does not have sword and ah chop up people; you have Bounty Killer and he is no killer, he nah kill nobody; Vybz Kartel is Daddy Devil, but Kartel is not no real devil; Mad Cobra he is not a snake; Elephant Man is no elephant. So why when I say I am Uncle Demon me ah real demon? Me not no real demon. ("I Am Not a Real Demon – Tommy Lee", *BVI News*, 2 February 2014)

Conceptualizing/Theorizing Gothic Dancehall

Originally, nineteenth-century gothic literature was associated exclusively with white aristocratic and middle-class Anglo-European men and a few women. Similarly, the gothic scene that later emerged in the United Kingdom in the 1980s was started by Anglo-European male artists. This indicates that the gothic literary genre and its later manifestations in twentieth-century Euro-America are the province of white upper- and middle-class men and women. However, in the twenty-first century, the goth/ic is a "multi-faceted, multi-dimensional force . . . a style, an aesthetic experience and a mode of cultural expression that transverses genres, forms, media, discipline and national boundaries" (Byron and Townshend 2014, xxxviii). Thus, contemporary goth/ic culture moves across contemporary popular culture into new spaces and places, giving rise to new incarnations. Spooner (2006, 8) asserts, "the Gothic lurks in all sorts of unexpected corners".

Like dancehall, Gothic aesthetics represent a watershed moment in popular music and cultural expressions of young Britons who rejected and rebelled against (white) elitist British nationalism. Being a cultural hybrid of the punk rock movement in the United Kingdom, goth/ic music is described as a subculture that came in response to the economic, social, cultural and nationalist upheavals in the United Kingdom during the 1980s (Mueller 2008).

However, goth has its point of origin in the popularity of the eighteenth- and nineteenth-century gothic literary genre. Gothic literary themes included, but were not limited to, death and decay, evil, the devil and Satan. The goth aesthetic re-emerged and reinvented itself from a literary genre in the form of subcultural expressions in fashion and music in the 1970s into the 1980s. Since the 1980s, gothic literary thematics, aesthetics and kinaesthetics (appearance and performance) have been incorporated in global popular cultures, in hip-hop music and culture, and Jamaica's own dancehall music and culture in the form of Tommy Lee Sparta.

It must be emphasized here that dancehall and goth have never coexisted in the same cultural space in Jamaica, although dancehall artistes and others, such as the late master dancer Gerald "Bogle" Levy, have always accessorized the physical body in spectacular and sartorial ways. This move towards what I label as gothic dancehall becomes a lyrical and metaphysical space where elements of dancehall music and culture intermingle with and are cross-fertilized by Afro-Jamaican religious folk culture and North American goth and *Twilight* culture. Gothic dancehall becomes dancehall's latest invention and is one of the ways the genre is able to re/present and re/invent itself. Here, gothic dancehall is a performative space where there is the cross-fertilization of music, embodied acts, repulsive shock and awe, visual body rhetoric, profiling, masquerading, Afro-Jamaican magico-religious rituals (such as sorcery and Obeah) and masking informed by dancehall body politics. As a hybrid, there is something at once sacred and profane about this new brand of dancehall having its antecedents not only in popular gothic music and culture but also in African traditions of masquerading and Jonkonnu. Jamaican Jonkonnu was practised as early as 1725 (Lewin 2000; Torres 2011) and featured characters such as Belly Woman and the Devil. The current flamboyant aesthetics and kinaesthetics of male dress and dancing styles in dancehall music and culture can be seen as the repressed traditions of Jonkonnu re/presenting themselves in transatlantic black cultures such as dancehall and hip-hop (Torres 2011). In this way, Euro-American gothic aesthetics and *Twilight* culture are similar to Afro-Jamaican rituals, beliefs and customs – for example, in their belief in magic, witchcraft, sorcery and exorcism. Thus, I posit that gothic dancehall, at the time of writing, is a space where historical and contemporary discourses overlap, intermingle and cross-fertilize in a reflective cycle of aesthetic sampling. These discourses include, but are not limited to, plantation entertainment and social dances, hybridization, transnationalism, globalization, free market capitalism, and the contemporary global wave of cinematic *Twilight*/gothic culture.

Tommy Lee Sparta as Uncle Demon

Tommy Lee emerged in 2008 in Montego Bay and performed at local shows in this part of Jamaica. However, he exploded into popular imagination one year after the first release of the *Twilight* trilogy, *The Twilight Saga: New Moon* in 2009 which was followed by *The Twilight Saga: Eclipse* in 2010 and *The Twilight Saga: Breaking Dawn* in 2012. Checks with Palace Amusement Company in Jamaica show that all three films had special premieres and were huge hits in the year of release. Where dark and gothic aesthetics are concerned, the rise of the *Twilight* series in popular cinema culture globally presents dark and light images and new ways of being in the contemporary era – new forms of identity-making for those who seek new platforms. In this era, therefore, Tommy Lee Sparta represents a new wave of artistes (including Ryme Minista, Gramma Stamma Sparta and the controversial Alkaline) whose aesthetic choices and self-presentations borrow from these gothic forms and are controversial in Jamaica's traditional sociocultural spaces.

Tommy Lee's explosion onto the dancehall stage in 2010 with his first hit "Warn Dem" was a new brand of dancehall signifying the kind of identity formation that transgresses traditional central themes of sex and sexuality, hyper-masculine heterosexuality, the lyrical/physical conquest of the pudenda, ghetto levity, and survival: this was the birth of the metaphorical Uncle Demon.[11] "Uncle Demon" must be analysed in its appropriate cultural climate: the moniker came at a time when movies such as *Twilight*, *300* and *Lord of the Rings*[12] had, arguably, normalized these dark, gothic figures who were transformed by feeling human emotions, having relationships, and being loving and affectionate. It could be that fans of Tommy Lee Sparta no longer felt threatened (real or imagined) by his embrace of a demonic moniker. Additionally, he came to prominence at a time when there was, arguably, a void in dancehall with the incarceration of Vybz Kartel and the perception that hardcore fans of dancehall were seeking something new, spectacular and controversial. While dancehall is used to controversy, one can argue that Tommy Lee Sparta rode a new wave of controversy by deliberately inflaming hegemonic structures and social institutions such as the monolithic Jamaican Christian orthodoxy. Yet this controversy was not initiated by Tommy Lee himself but by Vybz Kartel. Hope (2014) catalogues Vybz Kartel's wave of controversies, beginning with his lyrical and physical clash with veteran dancehall artiste Ninja Man at Sting 2003 (an annual dancehall music festival where artistes clash with one another lyrically). She further outlines Kartel's subsequent Gully/Gaza feud with arch-rival dancehall artiste Mavado, his normalization of fellatio, and his constant lyrical stabs at state and media entities such as the Broadcasting Commission, among others (Hope 2014). In this way, Tommy Lee Sparta became Vybz Kartel's (also self-styled as Daddy Devil) protégé of controversy, a wave now being ridden by Alkaline, another of dancehall's disruptive artistes.

Tommy Lee's highly charged and secular lyrics and his dabbling in "demonic" aesthetics were perceived by institutional authority and Jamaica's strong religious arm as a manifestation of the end of days and this perception travelled outwards into the wider Caribbean. This is exemplified in the responses to Tommy Lee's 2014 visit to Dominica, where one pastor described Tommy Lee as a threat to the safety of his entire nation. Tommy Lee Sparta's inflammatory brand of gothic dancehall was then laced with the images of demons or Satan and signalled an ideological/musical transition from "dangerous" dancehall to one of "dark/er dancehall". Indeed, at Tommy Lee's performance at Sting 2012 (his first appearance on dancehall's annual gladiatorial event, where artistes are lyrically crowned or dethroned), his costume incorporated gothic/demonic tropes, including a "demon" face mask and a long black leather coat, and his lyrics were of imprisonment, madness, monstrosity and haunting.

This radical move in dancehall aesthetics and performance at Sting 2012 generated intense controversy among fans and religious groups. Many wondered whether Tommy Lee Sparta was a part of the Illuminati or some secret society. Or was he the devil reincarnated or a beast from the book of Revelations? In Jamaican newspapers (for example, the *Jamaica Observer*, the *Daily Gleaner* and the *Star*) and on social media, as well as in discussions on the ground, debates centred around whether dancehall was being pushed too far and transgressing some of its own major tenets. Dancehall veterans were also critical. Ninja Man said: "In the name of Jesus, yuh affi rebuke the devil" (in the name of Jesus, you have to rebuke the devil), and Bounty Killer declared that "Christmas is fi Christ so nuh demon or devil cyaah win . . . dem a dead a Sting!!!" (Christmas is for Christ so no demon or devil can win . . . they are going to die at Sting) (Clarke 2012). Critics also included academics like Michael Barnett (2013), of the University of the West Indies at Mona, who argued in a conference presentation that "dancehall had lost its way".

I argue, however, that Tommy Lee Sparta's transgression was not only inflammatory but pointed to a new, cross-fertilized hybrid identity in the dancehall – a hardcore man who uses the dark, gothic *Twilight* images associated with demons as cultural referents. This updated hybrid on the stages of Jamaican dancehall has clear historical antecedents in images found in North American popular culture, starting with the likes of Marilyn Manson to Manson's hip-hop contemporaries Lil Wayne and Tyga, among others. While the persona of Uncle Demon is pulled from elements of American pop culture, Tommy Lee Sparta marries these with what Hope (2010) identifies as the don/shotta masculine identity[13] of dancehall music and culture. Thus, the persona of Tommy Lee Sparta as Uncle Demon was costumed with controversial and, for some, offensive imagery, including the four-leaf clover (which is believed to bring good luck), a fairy (one which has magical power and watches over subjects), the ankh (connected to ancient Egypt and a symbol of eternal life), the moon and the sun (which plays into the light/darkness dichotomy), and a swastika (originally associated with religions like Hinduism and Buddhism, but later German Nazism and its brutal regime that committed atrocities against humanity).

These body modifications and select costuming allowed Tommy Lee Sparta to brand his mundane self in hyper/visible and powerful ways that connect with Hollywood and North American moves in global cinema culture. Further, they helped to reposition and re/script him as part of the adopted persona of Uncle Demon and, along with the controversy surrounding him and "Daddy Devil" (that is, Vybz Kartel), to "accrue significantly greater cultural power" inna di dancehall. Using this artifice and self-presentation, Tommy Lee Sparta became a "celebrity figure . . . an object of public attention because he was perceived to embody possibilities of individual achievement; conversely, he also represents deviation from religious and social norms" (Bhattacharya 2012, para 4). His hyper/visible body was created in ways similar to those used by North American celebrities who sensationalize themselves by sartorial choices and body markings – for example, Lil' Wayne, Tyga and Thomas Lee Bass of the metal band Motley Crue. Additionally, Tommy Lee's lyrical treatises converged with his adornment and costuming to project him as the deviant Uncle Demon.

Tommy Lee's Lyrical Deviance

A careful examination of Tommy Lee's lyrical repertoire up to 2014 suggests that it can be catalogued under several major themes (see Campbell 2013): first, there is the description, critique or endorsement of acts of violence; second, sexual encounters, prowess and taboos; third, harmonious and dissonant interpersonal relationships; fourth, socio-economic/sociopolitical struggles of Jamaica's marginalized groups; fifth, ghetto/inner-city strategies of day-to-day survival; sixth, the general ways of entertaining oneself; and finally, the recognition of a supreme entities (God/Satan) in daily life. These lyrical themes tie directly into Hope's (2011, 19–23) identification and description of the "six G's and others" as key themes in contemporary dancehall music and culture – that is, gun, gyal, ghetto, gays, ganja, God and money/bling.

Following on the trajectory of many hardcore dancehall artistes like Ninja Man, the "Front Teeth, Gold Teeth Gun Pon Teeth Don Gorgon"; Super Cat, the Wild Apache; Bounty Killer, the Warlord; and Vybz Kartel, the Teacher, Tommy Lee Sparta's inflammatory lyrics, dark and anti-Christ music videos coupled with Satan as a cultural referent as well as his overtly accessorized physical body positioned him as the incarnation of gothic dancehall. With his gothic aesthetic sampling, Tommy Lee Sparta gave a fresh energy and power to contemporary dancehall. He crossed the soundscape of Montego Bay to become a part of the Portmore Empire, and burst into prominence, upsetting some while becoming the object of attention of many others. His songs like "Warn Dem" (November 2010) was followed by "Some Bwoy: Link Pan Wi Chain" (October 2011), and then with "Psycho" (June 2012), "Bus a Blank" (October 2012) and later "Shook (Uncle Demon)". Most of his songs, live performances and music videos rely heavily on gothic tropes to convey the intensity of terror and pain. A few are examined below.

"Uncle Demon", as is referenced in his songs, is a creation, an alter-ego who appears and disappears at will. Staged identities are important variants within the dancehall space and form part of becoming a successful and relevant artiste. Unlike other members of Vybz Kartel's Gaza Empire who were/are unable to access the upper echelons of dancehall music and culture (for example, Gaza Slim, Lisa Hyper and Jah Vinci), Tommy Lee Sparta discovered a "winning formula" with his creation of gothic dancehall and its complementary lyrics. For example, in "Psycho", Tommy Lee Sparta inverts one dimension of being Uncle Demon, "man psycho", thus:

> Dem nuh bad, act dem a act
> Talk dem a talk, dem a chat
> A Tommy Lee me a talk from me heart
> Wid bere badness back a dat
> Hmmmmmm hmmmmmmm hmmmmmm
> Man Psycho
> Gaza run bout yaaa
> Fool. . . .
>
> They are not bad, they are acting
> They are talking, they are chatting
> This is Tommy Lee, I am talking from my heart
> With pure badness to back it up
> Hmmmmmm hmmmmmmm hmmmmmm
> I am psycho
> Gaza controls here
> Fool. . . .

Tommy Lee Sparta announces his "madness" to the world and to his enemies and critics alike. This madness is as a result of being evil and about the violent and unfeeling ways that he would go about getting rid of an enemy "in front pastor, school pickney", that is, in front of a religious authority figure or a child in school (who should be protected from such things). In other words, a person would have to be mad/insane to be this violent. Tommy Lee (or the lyric persona) reinvents himself as an extraordinarily violent and unfeeling being, one who is more mad, loathsome, threatening and otherworldly than all others. The persona is more aggressive in lyrics, tempo and timbre. He tells his enemies in "Lucifer/Uncle Demon 2" about his destructive potential:

> Scream and cry to yo self
> Lord, call and run to yo God
> Nothing in this world could save yo
> Tonight you a dead like dog
> Aches to aches, dust to dust
> Like a wild pit bull mi bullet dem rus
> Shot kick yo in a yo face till yo fucking skull crush
> Any bwoy feel dem cyaa get touch
>
> Scream and cry to yourself
> Lord, call and run to your God
> Nothing in this world could save you
> Tonight you are going to die like a dog
> Ashes to ashes, dust to dust
> Like a wild pit bull my bullets will rush
> Shots will kick you in your face until your fucking skull is crushed
> Any boy who feels they can't get touched

This nihilistic projection becomes a haunting leitmotif for the lingering pain and terror that his enemies will endure as they are killed and buried. Here, Tommy Lee Sparta's lyric persona is the sorcerer/obeah man/obayifo who must be feared. Bastide (1972, 77) describes the general purpose of the obayifo/obeahman: "Their business is to prepare objects that are meant to kill or cure.... They can fly through the air, suck the blood of their victims, radiate light from their anus, and turn themselves into animals. They have a special connection to Satan." The lyric persona has mystical and magical but deadly powers. Thus, the lyric persona is angst-stricken and his tone is predominantly sinister, mysterious, haunting and monstrous.

In "Shook (Uncle Demon)", Tommy Lee Sparta announces the persona Uncle Demon and uses it as a reference point to demonstrate how he parallels the epitome of evil or badness associated with the devil and his legions:

Intro
Uncle demon
Nephew demon
Legion its uncle demon legion

Chorus

Any boy put a foot a get shook
Mi no care weh yo come from shook
Somebody head affi go open like boo
When mi walk a yo place an shot out yo face
Look in a yo marrow awe shook
God kill mi mi no have no heart
Mi evil than how mi blood cloth look
A mi first deh corrupt the war part
Legion

Intro
Uncle Demon
Nephew Demon
Legion, it's uncle demon, legion

Chorus

Any boy who puts a foot (out) is going to get shaken
I don't care where you are from, shook
Somebody's head is going to open like a book
When I walk over to your place and shoot out your face
(And) Look in your marrow, awe, shook
God strike me down, I don't have any heart
I am more evil than how I bloodcloth look
It was I who first corrupted the war path
Legion

While mentioning the name Uncle Demon and using the word *legion*, in this song, Tommy Lee Sparta is more particularly playing into the broader trajectory of evil/warrior/violent masculinities that make the round of Jamaican popular music, especially dancehall. What is clear is that he uses the demon/ic references to identify his ultimate degree of badness (violence) on a metaphysical plane, as he reminds his foes of his awesome power and simultaneously mocks the structures of power espoused by them: "Dem nuh bad, non a dem bwoy de nuh bad / Dem no bad like we, dem bwoy de no bad" (They are not bad, none of those boys are bad / They are not as bad as we, those boys are not bad). Here, the badness/violence which Tommy Lee Sparta mentions is other-worldly, one that is metaphysical, far beyond the ordinary. In this instance, Tommy Lee endorses and plays into the gun/violence, don/shotta dichotomies within the dancehall specifically and within the wider Jamaican society. He suggests that other than mere guns and human foot-soldiers, he is equipped with far more powerful and extremely violent entities as part of his brand of badness – that is, duppies and Satan, beings beyond this realm that cannot be defeated by humans. In this regard, Campbell (2013, 3) notes that "in fact, the demonic references seem to be directly related to this attempt at showing how psycho he is why 'dem nuh bad like a we'" (they are not as bad as we are). Indeed, during careful examination of Tommy Lee's lyrical output up to the time of writing, none of his songs mention Satan, demons or legions as entities to be worshipped or praised, but these form part of his larger meta-narrative about his legitimacy as successor to throne of the Gaza Empire (though some argue that it no longer exists in light of Kartel's incarceration) and as a new hybrid who is now a gladiator of dancehall music and culture. As the Gaza Empire is disrupted, Tommy Lee Sparta brands Montego Bay into prominence by creating a new empire.

The point should be made that the foregoing was Tommy Lee Sparta's attempt to advance to the highest ranks of lyrical gladiatorship in dancehall culture. His later retreat from the same and from the Uncle Demon moniker came in response to the backlash he received from within and beyond the dancehall. Jamaica and the Caribbean are locked within the strong fundamentalist Christian mores that view delving into spiritual other-worldliness as evil. Consequently, Tommy Lee Sparta moved away from the Uncle Demon moniker and its related lyrical output because of the backlash he received from various agenda setters and authority figures in the dancehall, media, in Jamaica and the wider Caribbean. For example, in a 2014 interview, he spoke about the pressures he was then facing from security forces that represented the face of the hegemonic governing structures in Jamaica. His retreat should also be understood in light of the arrest and later conviction of Vybz Kartel. The conviction of Vybz Kartel for murder in 2014 was seen as a return to law and order for many in Jamaica. Dancehall artistes associated with Vybz

Kartel were heavily policed as well. In one instance, Tommy Lee was blocked from performing at Sumfest 2015 because it was believed he posed a threat to the safety of the event and its environs. As at the time of writing, he has not been granted a US visa, thus limiting his international reach in North America, and is currently unable to break into corporate Jamaica to secure sponsorships or endorsements.

Conclusion

Dancehall espouses an informal set of collective beliefs and articulates problems associated with Jamaica's poor black majority. As a form of Jamaica popular culture, it continues to clash with the vanguards of morality and decency in Jamaica. The cultural dissonance of the late 1970s into the 1980s (Meeks 1996) created a space for ordinary Jamaicans to become extraordinary, such as the controversial Vybz Kartel. Tommy Lee Sparta's later alliance with Vybz Kartel, an artiste who continues to ride his own waves of controversy (now from behind bars), aided his meteoric rise between 2010 and 2014, particularly since Vybz Kartel has been physically absent from the dancehall stages since his arrest in 2009.

The rise of Tommy Lee Sparta as a gothic dancehall artiste was deliberately engineered around the marrying of global popular culture and the controversial themes in dancehall music and culture. His aesthetic ruptured conventional dancehall themes and challenged Jamaica's traditional moral and religious foundations. Like his mentor, Vybz Kartel, Tommy Lee Sparta became the object of public scrutiny within and beyond the shores of Jamaica and the Caribbean (up to 2014). His controversial popular cultural moments raised concerns about his influence on the youth and the wider public, even while the society continued to face significant challenges from rising rates of crime and violence and indiscipline among teenagers, among other issues.

Tommy Lee Sparta's aesthetic sampling is a revolt against the strictures of Jamaica's religiosity and the traditional mores used to police Jamaican popular music and culture. Since 2014, Tommy Lee Sparta's retreat from the public domain as Uncle Demon has had a serious impact on his career as the awe that he originally generated has waned. The spectacular costumes and inflammatory lyrics of dancehall culture's celebrity-making processes continue to clash with the moral and ethical constraints of contemporary Jamaican society.

Notes

1. *Twilight* is a young-adult vampire-romance novel by Stephenie Meyer (2005) that formed the basis of the successful film adaptation in 2008 which shows images of vampires and other gothic creatures such as wolves. Vampires are usually portrayed as scary and evil but *Twilight* romaticizes and sanitizes vampirism, making it attractive to Jamaican youth and others. The word *twilight* itself is a hybrid of light and darkness meeting at an intersection.
2. The word *smaddy* (root/route word of *smadditization*) is the Jamaican Creole for "somebody". The concept and process of "smadditization" is accredited to cultural scholar and intellectual giant Rex Nettleford. However, it was originally used by the late Tony Laing, popular Jamaican arts consultant and talk show host, who characterized the 1970s as the period of "smadditization". It was a time when Jamaicans from "below" or lower classes were invigorated by a sharper sense of personhood than ever before in Jamaica's twentieth-century history (see Nettleford 1998, 259). "Smadditization" should also be seen as a continuous process by dancehall artistes to re-engineer or re/create the ordinary self to the sensational and the spectacular, or, in the case of Tommy Lee Sparta, the grotesque.
3. Jamaica's popular musical etymology is catalogued in the works of Donna Hope (2001, 2006a, 2006b), Sonjah Stanley Niaah (2010) and Carolyn Cooper (1993), among others.
4. Vybz Kartel is considered to be a protégé of veteran dancehall artiste Bounty Killer. Bounty Killer is credited with introducing Vybz Kartel to the dancehall industry in 2001 at a dancehall event, Reloaded, in Portmore, St Catherine. Vybz Kartel is considered one of a new generation of artistes (including Wayne Marshall) who emerged at the beginning of the twenty-first century with a distinct sound, lyrical prowess and vocalizing abilities. His controversial moments in and outside of dancehall include the Gully/Gaza feud with rival dancehall artist Mavado; his banned song "Rampin Shop" (2009), featuring dancehall artist Spice; and his ultimate arrest and murder conviction (along with three co-accuseds) in 2014. He is currently serving a thirty-five-year sentence for murder before being eligible for parole.
5. In an interview with the researcher on 21 September 2014, Tommy Lee Sparta stated that he was very popular in Montego Bay but it was Vybz Kartel, hav-

ing invited him to relocate to Kingston, who brought him to dancehall/musical consciousness in the imagination of dancehall fanatics.

6. Arguably mimicking the persona of Ninja Man, another dancehall legend of the late 1980s into the early 1990s, Bounty Killer emerged during the golden era of dancehall music when many new artistes came onto the dancehall scene and mounted successful careers. Now a dancehall veteran, Bounty Killer emerged in the dancehall in the 1990s as the "Poor People Governer" with his Dave Kelly–penned hit songs such as "Anytime" (1999) and "Fed Up" (1996) that spoke critically to issues of social justice and poverty. He is a multifaceted and multidimensional artist who belongs to the upper echelons of dancehall music and culture and who is credited for bringing forth the most new dancehall artistes.

7. Urbanization is the process by which large portions of a population migrate from rural to urban areas. Jamaica has seen its wave of urbanization, as is captured in the movie *The Harder They Come* (1972) where Ivanhoe Martin, the protagonist played by Jimmy Cliff, leaves his rural home when his grandmother dies to live in the inner cities of Kingston with his mother. This was his attempt at getting meaningful employment but he could not eke out a living and so turned to a life of crime. Waves of rural to urban migration continued into the 1980s, 1990s and 2000s to other parts of Jamaica, including St Catherine (especially Portmore), St James (for example, Montego Bay) and St Andrew. This resulted also in the spread of inner cities in these areas as social and economic pressures presented survival challenges for the poor. Vybz Kartel from Portmore, St Catherine, and Tommy Lee Sparta from Montego Bay, St James, are the children of migrants to the urban areas. They represent a new generation of lyrical griots who demand a space in dancehall music and culture.

8. The word *buss* in dancehall means "burst" or to get a break in the musical space, to become popular. This means that the individual artiste has a popular song that leads to real rewards, such as bookings for popular dancehall events. One should note, however, that getting a buss does not always translate into fame or long-term economic rewards.

9. The phrase *inna di dancehall* means "in the dancehall". This means all the activities that are taking place within the cultural and musical space of dancehall – for example, the latest trends in fashion and so on. The phrase was originally the title of a chapter in the book *Reggae Routes* (Chang and Chen 1998), written as "Inna the Dancehall". The phrase was later adopted and adapted by popular culture scholar Donna Hope (2006a) in her book *Inna Di Dancehall: Popular Culture and the Politics of Identity in Jamaica*.

10. Keith Shebada Ramsay is a popular roots-theatre actor who plays androgynous

or feminized roles. In the dancehall, he is considered a homosexual, a masculine identity that is negated in this music and culture. Because of the use of the word *borderline* by Keith Shebada Ransay in his play *Bashment Granny*, suggesting that he was neither man nor woman, dancehall gladiator Vybz Kartel felt the need to change the name of his community to distance himself as well his community from a perceived homosexual.

11. In my informal interviews with Tommy Lee Sparta, he explained that the moniker Uncle Demon was the name of his then manager, Junior "Heavy D" Fraser. He explained that one day when he was in the studio recording, someone came and asked for Uncle D, that is, Heavy D. The individual stated, "Weh Uncle D mon deh?" which translates to mean "Where is Uncle D, the man?" Tommy Lee Sparta stated that since that incident, the moniker Uncle Demon became associated with him and he decided to embrace it, even though the moniker was for his then manager and not himself.

12. The movies *300* and *Lord of the Rings* are not considered traditional gothic movies. However, they are relevant to discussions about gothic aesthetics emerging in Jamaica at the time of writing. Both movies borrow certain dark images from gothic fiction and are laden with gothic trappings (creepy and dark settings), the uncanny (strange and supernatural beings) and supernatural forces (such as the ring of power having the capacity to save and or damn Earth and associated worlds).

13. The don/shotta masculine identity is routed/rooted in a Machiavellian male figure who commands respect but is also feared by others. This variant of masculinity is linked to violence and aggression and uses the gun in song lyrics and on stage as a powerful and explosive weapon. In her discussions on cultural manifestations of masculinity, Donna Hope (2001, 2006a, 2010) argues that this variant is linked to aggression as a component of Jamaica's sociocultural manifestations of hegemonic lower-class masculinity.

References

Barnett, Michael. 2013. "Has Dancehall Lost Its Way or Have We Merely Transitioned to a Post-Dancehall Era?" Paper presented at the International Reggae Conference, University of the West Indies, Mona. 14–16 February.

Bastide, Roger. 1972. *African Civilizations in the New World*. Harper and Row.

Bhattacharya, Saradindu. 2012. "Demons and Demos: Voldemort, Democracy and Celebrity Culture". *Looking Glass* 16 (1).http://www.lib.latrobe.edu.au/ojs/index.php/tlg/article/view/279/276.

Byron, Glennis, and Dale Townshend. 2014. *The Gothic World*. Routledge.

Campbell, Winston. 2013. "The Collective Opuses of Tommy Lee Sparta: A Theoretical Response". Paper presented at the International Reggae Conference, University of the West Indies, Mona. 14–16 February.

Chang, Kevin O'Brien, and Wayne Chen. 1998. *Reggae Routes: The Story of Jamaican Music*. Kingston: Ian Randle.

Clarke, Curtis. 2012. "Bounty Lashes out at Tommy Lee: Others Also Voice Concern about Demonic Songs". *Star*, 11 September.

Cooper, Carolyn. 1993. *Noises in the Blood: Orality, Gender, and the "Vulgar" Body of Jamaican Popular Culture*. London: Macmillan.

———. 2004. *Sound Clash: Jamaican Dancehall Culture from Lady Saw to Dancehall Queen*. London: Palgrave Macmillan.

Hall, Stuart. 1979. "The Great Moving Right Show". *Marxism Today* (January): 14–20.

Hope, Donna P. 2001. "Inna di Dancehall Dis/Place: Sociocultural Politics of Identity in Jamaica". MPhil thesis, University of the West Indies.

———. 2006a. *Inna Di Dancehall: Popular Culture and the Politics of Identity in Jamaica*. Kingston: University of the West Indies Press.

———. 2006b. "Passa Passa: Interrogating Cultural Hybridities in Jamaican Dancehalls". In *Small Axe*, no. 21 (October): 119–33.

———. 2010. *Man Vibes: Masculinities in the Jamaican Dancehall*. Kingston: Ian Randle.

———. 2011. "Dancehall: Origins, History, Future". *Groundings*, no. 26 (July): 7–28.

———. 2014. "The Kartel Phenomenon: Popular Culture and the Culture of Celebrity in Jamaican Dancehall". Paper presented at the Institute of Cultural Studies seminar series, University of the West Indies, Mona, 11 April.

Lewin, Olive. 2000. *"Rock It Come Over": The Folk Music of Jamaica*. Kingston: University of the West Indies Press.

Meeks, Brian. 1996. "The Political Moment in Jamaica: The Dimensions of Hegemonic Dissolution". In *Dispatches from the Ebony Tower: Intellectuals Confront the African American Experience*, edited by Manning Marable, 52–74. New York: Columbia University Press.

Mueller, Charles Allen. 2008. "The Music of the Goth Subculture: Postmodernism and Aesthetics". PhD dissertation, Florida State University.

Nettleford, Rex. 1998. *Mirror Mirror: Identity, Race and Protest in Jamaica*. Kingston: LMH Publishing.

Spooner, Catherine. 2006. *Contemporary Gothic*. London: Reaktion Books.

Stanley-Niaah, Sonjah. 2005. "'Dis Slackness Ting': A Dichotomizing Master Narrative in Jamaican Dancehall". *Caribbean Quarterly* 51 (3–4): 55–76.

———. 2010. *Dancehall: From Slave Ship to Ghetto*. Ottawa: University of Ottawa Press.

Stolzoff, Norman. 2000. *Wake the Town and Tell the People: DancehallCulture in Jamaica*. Durham, NC: Duke University Press.

Torres, Lena Delgado de. 2011. "Swagga: Fashion, Kinaesthetics and Gender in Dancehall and Hip Hop". *Journal of Black Masculinity: The Philosophical Underpinnings of Gender Identity* 1 (3). http://www.blackmasculinity.com.

CHAPTER 3

THE DEVELOPMENT OF REGGAE MUSIC IN MEXICO
A Periodization of Its Adoption and Adaptation

CHRISTIAN EUGENIO LÓPEZ-NEGRETE MIRANDA

Does reggae music exist in Mexico? When and how did this genre of Jamaican music arrive in Mexico? Has adoption and adaptation allowed the emergence of a Mexican reggae? For a better understanding, we need to know a little about the sociocultural context in each of the periods of the development of reggae in Mexico, as well as other aspects such as the musicians and bands that are taken as a model and have more influence, along with the Mexicans musicians, bands and sound systems more representative of each period. In this way, we can see the discourses most frequently used and other important performative elements in order to detect the main issues addressed by reggae in Mexico – for example, the presence or absence of Rastafari content in each period. Here, I propose a periodization of the different moments of reggae in Mexico and Mexican reggae, historicizing and characterizing each period. It is important to note that the periodization I propose is a useful methodological tool for understanding the development of reggae music in Mexico; however, it also demonstrates the existence of a stream of Mexico-made music that, since the early 1960s, has had a great influence on Jamaican popular music.

This work is part of a larger ongoing research entitled "The Musical Scene of Reggae in Mexico: Expressions of Glocalization and Translocality" that seeks to explain the cultural particularities that Rastafari music expresses in Mexico and how these, in turn, enrich the global reggae scene. Reggae music in Mexico is a unique case, due, among other things, to the role of the Mexican Caribbean[1] and the adoption of these musical practices in a predominantly Spanish-speaking and Catholic context. In addition, the strong presence of an indigenous and a mestizo population rescuing its diluted African heritage has produced a self-expression that simultaneously maintains several characteristics of Rastafari music, mainly reggae music. This chapter provides empirical information for an understanding of the development, implications and impact of reggae in Mexico, which are issues of great relevance for studies of urban popular music. Thus, I offer a historical and analytical review of the Mexican reggae scene, a genre of popular music that, in Mexico, has rarely been studied. Understanding the value of reggae, like all other genres, lies in both its cultural function and its sound qualities (coupled with the perception of sound that has been crucial in the process of creation, dissemination, appreciation and enjoyment of reggae). I present a multidisciplinary approach to address the issue from different perspectives, based on a review of works from various disciplines.

In order to delimit the subject of study and have an axis that links all the aspects discussed, this chapter draws on the notion of *scene* as the basic unit in the delimitation of the study object (dispensing with the terms *subculture* and *counterculture*), derived from both the theorizing about this concept proposed by specialists from academia as well as the discourses of reggae fans themselves. Thus, the study of the reggae scene in Mexico is delimited, placing it in necessary relation to other musical practices, other stylistic and geographic realities, while forming an intersubjective, transnational perspective. The notion of *scene* has been used in journalism from the 1940s and in academia since the 1990s, and has taken root in popular culture as a commonly used term.

Cohen (1999) and Bennet and Peterson (1994) have provided important considerations about the concept of *scene* that are useful in introducing some of the fundamental ideas that I use, for example:

> The term is perhaps most often applied to groups of people and organizations, situations and events involved with the production and consumption of particular music genres and styles. (Cohen 1999, 239)

> The concept "music scene" ... is increasingly used by academic researchers to designate the contexts in which clusters of producers, musicians, and fans collectively share their common musical tastes and collectively distinguish themselves from others. (Bennett and Peterson 1994, 1)

In both definitions, considerations of collective activity and identification appear as the central characteristic of a scene, but this collective is not the scene; rather, it is a part of its activities, products, ideologies and other elements involved with the musical genre in question. In addition, there are groups without a clear delineation (linking through a musical genre can be flexible and imprecise) or stability (membership of a person to a particular scene can be subjective, admit varying degrees of intensity or change over time). In these respects, the concept of *scene* is clearly distinguished from *community*.

The scenes are made up of people who carry out activities from their interactions. The relations between these individuals can be of various types: information, warnings, gossip, questions about instruments, musical issues, magazines and recordings. Thus, the musician, the audience and the music-industry businessmen create various networks, cliques and factions, and the scene is divided by musical styles, classes, feuds, rivalries and other elements. The sites of these interactions are varied: music shops, rehearsal rooms, recording studios, concerts. Bennett and Peterson (1994, 1) give a similar definition of *scene*: "groups of producers, musicians and fans collectively share their common musical tastes, differing from other groups". Geographers John Connell and Chris Gibson (2001, 101) add other elements in their definition of *scene*: "there must be a critical mass for musicians and followers, a number of recording, interpretation and listening infrastructures: studios, rooms and even record companies and distribution points ... many of these spaces have emerged from subversive projects: appropriation of urban spaces for subcultural use, new independent media (like pirate radio) and places to hedonistic practice, as clubs and festivals".

Bennett and Peterson (1994, 7) expand the influence of local culture, pointing to the dialect as well as certain types of clothing or forms of local knowledge. Therefore, we must not ignore the aesthetic dimension of scenes. While we can find a taste for various musical genres in a scene, perhaps we can find some shared conventions and aesthetic forms (technical, theme in the lyrics, or ideological conceptions) shared by members of the scene.

As suggested by Bennett and Peterson (1994, 12), scene boundaries tend to be imprecise. In this chapter, we have taken reggae music as the core of this scene and Mexico as a general geographical area. But this does not mean that this scene does not involve other types of music or that it includes only what happens within the political boundaries of the country; in fact, this study would not be possible without considering other musical practices and other stylistic and geographic realities. Certainly, it is not meant to imply that there is a unique reggae scene in Mexico characterized by the inclusion of a number of elements and discarding others; it is, rather, a multiple reality, the definition changes depending on the approach considered in each moment. The scene concept incorporates aesthetic elements in its definition, and in its conceptualization it is linked to the spaces where the scenes take place, as well as historical, cultural and social elements that surround these scenes and of which these are a part. Therefore, we can understand that within reggae are multiple scenes, and among these there are exchange relations and even competitive relations between each other. In this regard, it is important to mention the work of Fernández (2012) on the ska scene in Spain because of its useful application to the case of the reggae scene in Mexico.

Using the foregoing as a platform, let us examine my proposal of a periodization of the development of reggae music in Mexico to locate different times, stages or waves, which are distinguished from each other. This periodization allows us to examine how the processes of categorization work in identifying various types of reggae and the stylistic features considered characteristic of each. It also serves to clarify the types of reggae that have developed in the Mexican context, the practices or assimilated features from foreign reggae that have prevailed on local reggae, and the features that have been rejected or have gained less fame. To facilitate the understanding of the content, and based on the information collected, I established six periods in the development of reggae in Mexico that, although subsequently could be modified or adjusted slightly with subsequent findings of this research, are useful: the previous period, 1960–69; the first period, 1970–79; the transition period, 1980–86; the second period, since 1987; the third period, since 2000; and the fourth period, since 2010.

CHRISTIAN EUGENIO LÓPEZ-NEGRETE MIRANDA

A Proposed Periodization of Reggae in Mexico

It is critical that we distinguish between reggae in Mexico and Mexican reggae. The first is made up of all the elements that make up the reggae music scene globally and that could be accessed in Mexico. These include radio stations with programmes dedicated to reggae music; concerts of reggae superstars from countries such as Jamaica, the United Kingdom and the United States; the sale of original reggae albums in major music stores; and covers and Spanish versions of great hits of famous musicians like Bob Marley or Byron Lee. So, there are different ways and places to acquire, approach or even interpret reggae in Mexico. Speaking of reggae in Mexico is to speak not only of its presence but also the adoption of this genre in a different context.

Second, Mexican reggae is formed from all the elements that compose this scene at national and local levels, which can generate various adaptations of reggae from different interpretations. For example, Mexican reggae began to mix and merge the characteristic elements and rhythmic patterns of reggae and other styles of Jamaican popular music with Mexican folk and traditional music. Sometimes traditional Mexican musical instruments such as clay ocarinas or the *jarana jarocha*[2] are incorporated into reggae that addresses local social and cultural issues in the lyrics. In a few cases, lyrics are sung in indigenous languages like Nahuatl or Maya. So there are different ways in which Mexican reggae is expressed. Therefore, when we speak of Mexican reggae, we mean a process of adaptation that goes beyond the adoption of this genre. Consequently, the development of Mexican reggae is part of the history of reggae in Mexico.

Since the arrival of reggae in Mexico early in the 1970s, we can identify different stages that are distinguished by different aspects. The main issues used in this work to characterize each period are as follows: the predominant style of reggae; the musicians and bands that are taken as a model and have more influence; the presence of Rastafari in the lyrical themes; and the Mexicans musicians, bands and sound systems that are representative of each period. In this way we can propose four distinct periods of reggae in Mexico from the 1970s, a previous period from the 1960s as well as an intermediate or transitional period in the 1980s occurring just after the first period and before the emergence of the Mexican reggae.

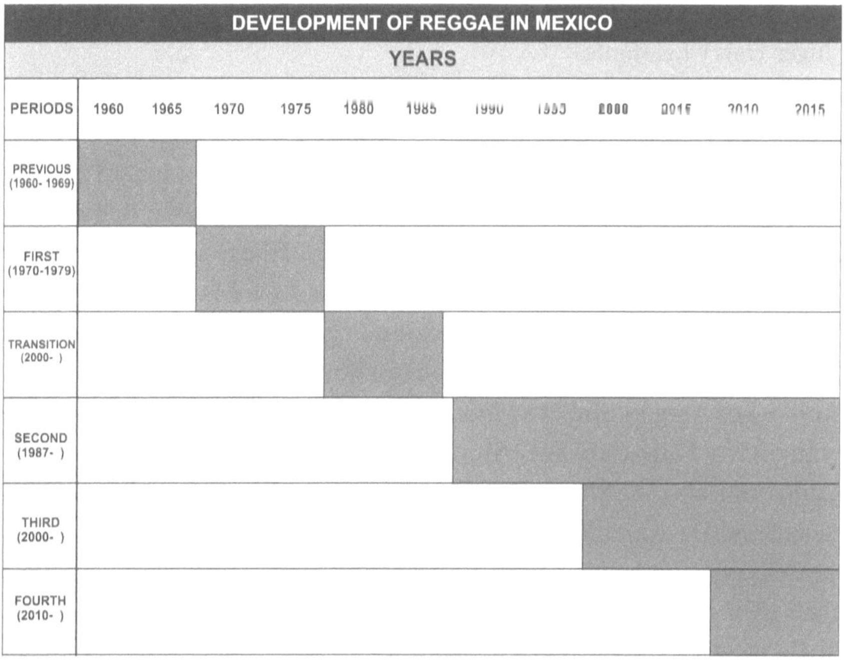

THE DEVELOPMENT OF REGGAE MUSIC IN MEXICO

FIGURE 3.1. Periodization of reggae in Mexico

The chart in figure 3.1 illustrates the six periods, which will each be subsequently discussed in more detail.

Previous Period (1960–1969)

From the middle of the 1940s and until the late 1950s, there were several Cuban musical genres in Mexico, such as mambo, rumba, guaguancó among others, that were successful and diffused thanks to the Mexican cinema of the time. So-called tropical music[3] was so popular among the Mexican audience that it became the music with the most presence in the discography and on national radio. The predecessor or prior period marks the arrival of Jamaican popular music to Mexico as a combination of "tropical music" with rock 'n' roll. This era probably began with the song "Bote de Bananas" (1961) by Los Rebeldes del Rock, a pioneering Mexican rock 'n' roll group who made the Spanish version of the traditional Jamaican folk song in mento style "Day-O (The Banana Boat Song)" (1956) done by African American singer Harry Belafonte.

Shortly after, around 1965, Mexican musician Toño Quirazco was commissioned by Discos Orfeón, the label where he worked, to go to Jamaica and learn the rhythm known as ska that had become so popular. After witnessing the most representative ska bands, Quirazco brought this rhythm back with him to Mexico, incorporating the use of the Hawaiian guitar. The involvement of different bands on the television show *Discotheque Orfeon a Go-gó*[4] was important in spreading ska among the Mexican audience. Thus, bands like Toño Quirazco y sus Hawaiian Boys, Los Yorsy's, Los Socios del Ritmo, Los Aragón, and Los Moonlights spread Jamaican music in Mexico with covers of musicians like Byron Lee and the Dragonnaires, the Skatalites, Carlos Malcolm, the Maytals, the Blues Busters, the Baba Brooks Band, Millie Small, and Dave and Ansel Collins, among others. In addition to Spanish versions of major Jamaican hits, musicians like Toño Quirazco popularized their own compositions, such as "Ska hawaiano", "Xalapa Ska", "Mérida Ska", "Ska Chihuahua" and "Ska Monterrey". However, towards the end of the 1960s, Quirazco also ventured into rhythms like boogaloo. The music industry managed ska in Mexico as part of the rock 'n' roll scene, which lost prominence at the end of the decade with the emergence of Mexican rock.

First Period (1970–1979)

Due to a strong intercultural relationship between Chetumal, in Quintana Roo, and Belize, one can observe that in the late 1960s, Belize (then known as British Honduras) was the gateway for reggae music to Mexico through Chetumal, along with other Belizean musical genres such as brukdown and punta. However, the style of reggae music that arrived and influenced its development in Mexico was a reggae coming out of the rocksteady era known as early reggae or reggay (with much influence from Afro-American soul and funk music). This predates the strong linkage between reggae music and the Rastafari movement of the roots reggae in the 1970s. By observing the number of covers made by Mexican bands, we can see that Byron Lee and the Dragonnaires, Calypso Rose, Ken Lazarus, Lord Kitchener, and Toots and the Maytals were the musicians who most influenced the sound

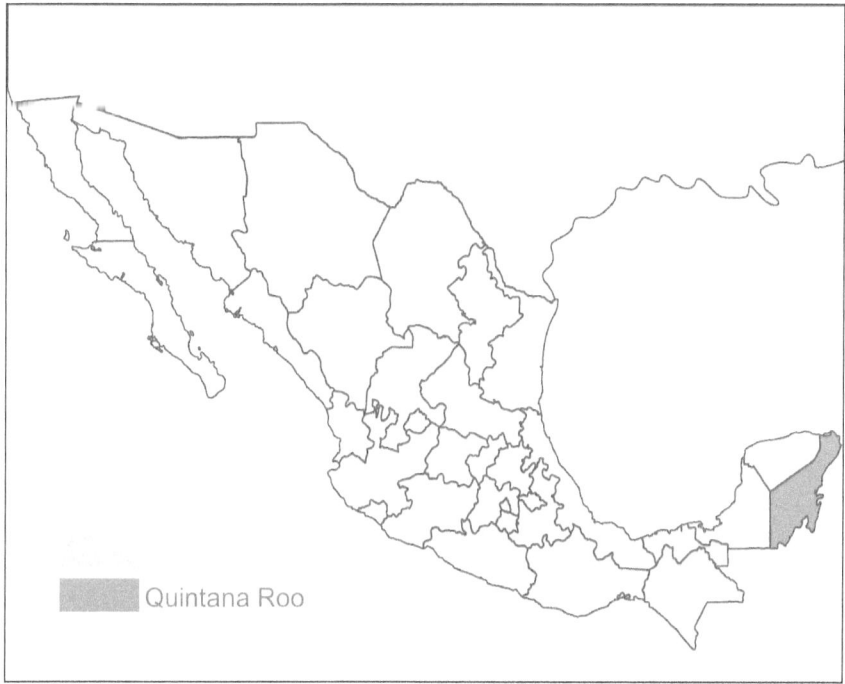

FIGURE 3.2. Map of Mexico, highlighting the state of Quintana Roo located in the southeast of the country in the area known as the Mexican Caribbean, where the first reggae bands appeared in the country; and Mexico City, the main focus of the reggae scene in Mexico since the early 1990s.

of the initial reggae made in Mexico. The emergence of a scene in Chetumal gave rise to two bands considered today as the pioneers of reggae in Mexico: Benny y su Grupo and Ely Combo. These bands mixed genres like calypso, soca and ska with reggae and represent the first period of reggae in Mexico, both through their versions of famous songs from Belize or Jamaica and through their own compositions with their particular style and flavour of the Mexican Caribbean (López-Negrete 2013, 10–15).

The sounds of early reggae gave way to a more elaborate sound and this period seems to culminate with the launch of the album *Catch a Fire* by the Wailers in 1973 and the adoption of the rhythm known as *one-drop* on the drums of reggae. At the same time, the creation of the state of Quintana Roo in 1974 corresponds with the dilution of Afro-Caribbean music in the national project. The territory that became the state of Quintana Roo, however, did not comply with one of the legal requirements for obtaining the status of state – that is, to have more than eighty thousand inhabitants. Because of this, the federal government implemented an immigration policy to attract people from different states of the country.[5] This policy was complemented by the arrival of Belizean and Caribbean music to Chetumal, when new inhabitants brought their customs and their music. As a result, local musicians began to include other genres in their repertoire and began gradually to put aside reggae music. Historically, the Mexican Caribbean represents the gateway of reggae to the rest of the country, and it generated a particularly local reggae scene in the state of Quintana Roo that was pioneering in the development of this genre in the country. In addition, the Mexican Caribbean has significantly influenced the meeting of musicians and the emergence of bands that later give rise to the following periods focused primarily on Mexico City.

Transition Period (1980–1986)

With Bob Marley and the Wailers reaching the pinnacle of popularity in Europe and the United States from 1973, reggae was already known in certain Mexican youth circles during the 1970s. Although the mainstream media achieved greater visibility for the music, the micro-diffusion generated by individual travellers to Mexico with new musical proposals was always significant, especially when they were included in alternative communication channels.

During the second half of the 1970s and most of the 1980s, reggae in Mexico was present through popular reggae albums that were published in the country and the performances of a few foreign bands, such as the concert by the Police (an English band with a strong reggae influence) in Mexico City in 1980. It is important to note that during this period, Mexican rock developed, marked by the Avándaro Festival in 1971,[6] the appearance of the hoyos fonquis (funky holes),[7] the underground scene and, subsequently, the implementation by the record label companies of the stream of *Rock en tu Idioma* (Rock in your Language).[8] In this context, in spite of the restrictions imposed in Mexico favouring linguistic and culturally Spanish-speaking productions and with fewer sociopolitical implications, several Mexican rock bands and musicians like Eduardo "Rosario" Duarte (1971), Ritmo Peligroso (1978), Sombrero Verde (hoy Maná) (1981), Maldita Vecindad y los Hijos del Quinto Patio (1985), Tex Tex (1986) and El Personal (1987), among others, began adding some elements of reggae to their performances and, although they were not reggae musicians, began to incorporate some original songs with a reggae beat in their albums. Another important element is the appearance of the first radio programme dedicated to reggae music in Mexico in the mid-1980s: *Off Beat*, hosted by Cecilia Perez Gasga and Dominique Peralta on Rock 101 FM. For more than ten years (1985–96), this represented a milestone in Mexican radio, introducing many of the great artists and bands of Jamaican reggae and its subgenres, and becoming an important reference for the next generation of programmes dedicated to this genre on other radio stations, such as *Reggae Beat*, *Aguas de Jamaica* and *Reggae y Algo Más*.

Second Period (1987–1999)

Mexican reggae itself is believed to appear in the second period, 1987–1999. Carolina Benavente mentions that the effective connection with the Caribbean was still marginal in those years. In Mexico City, for example, there are those who recall the existence of a cassette with "music from Jamaica", introduced by a Haitian doctor who emigrated towards the end of the 1970s and, later, in Guadalajara, the influence of remaining Brazilians is also added in the country after the World Cup of 1986. By the end of the 1980s, the connection became more concrete, with performances by the Jamaican reggae band Chalice at the Cervantino Festival in Guanajuato and in the National Auditorium in Mexico City. In Cancun, Quintana Roo, reggae was elaborated on a symbolic combination of beach and rock that was decisive in its later evolution (Benavente 2005, 5). This is where one of the first Mexican reggae bands was created in this period: the Splash band formed around 1982 and they are now regarded as a pioneer of Mexican reggae in this period. Splash was the first Mexican reggae band that played in Jamaica at Reggae Sunsplash in 1990, and the band even participated in the organization of the first Sunsplash Festival in Mexico City at Atlante Stadium in the same year. Due to the work of people like the Mexican-Dutch reggae promoter Monica Kessler in the early 1990s, the north of Quintana Roo became a kind of school for Mexican reggae (Enríquez 2014, 42).

Consequently, there developed other bands with musicians from the capital country like Blitz, Los Olvidados, La Flota and Signos Distantes (which broke up and gave rise to Bosquimano and Selah). In addition, in the early 1990s, there began to develop a movement around reggae music in Mexico City led by bands like Rastrillos (1989), Yerberos (1992) and Antidoping (formerly Selah) (1992). These bands were heavily influenced by musicians like Bob Marley and the Wailers, Burning Spear, Black Uhuru, Israel Vibration, Jacob Miller, Jimmy Cliff, Steel Pulse, the Gladiators, and Third World, who all belonged to the era of reggae known as roots reggae and rockers. These Mexican reggae bands organized the Razteca Festival in 1993, which was the first reggae festival in Mexico that aimed to connect the Mexican indigenous knowledge and social protest with what was known about the Rastafari movement through the lyrics of Jamaican reggae.[9] However, Mexican reggae was still so marginal that not even Off Beat included it in their programming. It is important to note that some of the bands of this period began to incorporate mentions of Rastafari in some songs from their first albums; in addition to references to national sociopolitical conflicts as the indigenous uprising of the Zapatista Army of National Liberation,[10] the economic crisis and other aspects of the social situation prevailing in the country such as violence, poverty and unemployment, often alluding to an internal and individual revolution that generates social changes. Here are a couple of examples:

> **Rastrillos, "Latinoamericana Revolution" (1992)**
> Latinoamericana Revolution
> Latinoamericanos Revolution
> Latinoamericana Revolution
> Siempre había pensado que estas cosas no iban a suceder
> Un estallido de bomba de forma casual
> El que tiene poder y usa violencia
> También se encuentra con la violencia
> Veinte muertos, no más
> Veinte muertos rezan los diarios

Nosotros sabemos que fueron más!
También encuentran violencia
Muchos hermanos latinos que viven a diario actos de terror
En sus calles no existe tranquilidad
Ninguna felicidad hay en sus corazones
Cuando han perdido a alguien
Cuando han perdido a alguien inocente
Oye, oye, oye hay que abrir los ojos
Vamos a regresar a las sensaciones
Salirnos del simulacro
Salirse del simulacro en que estamos viviendo
Porque no debemos alimentar esta vaga ilusión
Porque no podrán detener esta revolución interior
Oh Babylon!
Latinoamericana Revolution
Latinoamericana Revolution
Latinoamericanos Revolution

Rastrillos, "Latin American Revolution" (1992)
Latin American Revolution
Latin Americans Revolution
I had always thought that these things were not going to happen
A bomb exploding in a casual manner
The one who has power and uses violence
He also encounters violence
Twenty dead, no more
Twenty dead newspapers pray
We know that we were more!
Also they find violence
Many Latino brothers who live daily acts of terror
In its streets there is no tranquility
No happiness is in their hearts
When they have lost someone
When they have lost someone innocent
Hey, hey, hey you have to open your eyes
Let's get back to the sensations
Leave the simulacrum
To leave the simulacrum in which we are living
Because we should not feed this vague illusion

Because they cannot stop this inner revolution
Oh Babylon!
Latin American Revolution
Latin American Revolution
Latin Americans Revolution

Antidoping, "La Solución" (1996)
Mira lo que está pasando
Oye lo que está ocurriendo
La gente se está matando
En las calles de la ciudad
Luchando por un pan
Por un pan
Mira lo que está pasando
Oye lo que está ocurriendo
Ríos de sangre te salpican
Y no haces nada!
Por evitarlo
La necesidad, nos agobia
Nos vuelve mendigos o ladrones
No te rindas, ni te pierdas
Abre tu corazón
Y mira adentro
Ahí está, ahí está
La solución, revolución
Es la revolución
En tu mente y en tu corazón
Por las calles de una nueva nación

Antidoping, "The Solution" (1996)
Look what's happening
Hear what is happening
People are killing themselves
On the streets of the city
Fighting for a loaf
For a loaf
Look what's happening
Hear what is happening
Rivers of blood splatter you

THE DEVELOPMENT OF REGGAE MUSIC IN MEXICO

And you do not do anything!
To avoid it
Need overwhelms us
It makes us beggars or thieves
Do not give up, do not lose
Open your heart
And look inside
There it is, there it is
The solution, revolution
It's the revolution
In your mind and in your heart
Through the streets of a new nation

The Razteca Festival had seven editions and enabled the creation of a network of Mexican reggae and the insertion of Mexico in the Latin American reggae scene. According to Gerardo Pimentel "Zopi" (interview with author, Mexico City, 1 August 2010), vocalist and bassist of the band Rastrillos and one of the founders and producers of the Razteca Festival, this network established communication with reggae bands from Puerto Rico, Argentina, Venezuela and Chile. It came to be regarded as the main reggae festival in Latin America and managed to define the direction of the movement, giving reggae a differentiated space from the Mexican *rock* scene. However, because of its great success, the fifth edition of the festival, in 2000 was held under the aegis of Operadora de Centros de Espectáculos S.A., a company owned by CIE (Inter American Entertainment Corporation), who obtained and legally registered the name "Razteca". The new situation of the festival was strongly criticized by the bands that gave it birth.

For many people, the Razteca Festival was about renewing Rastafari's vision under a new local cultural view, which explains the appeal to values of protest as well as a harmonious relationship with nature and an ecological conscience. As Gerardo Pimentel "Zopi" comments, many of the first bands sang about Rastafari in an intuitive way because there was not much information available and that made the interpretation of Rastafari in Mexico more flexible. In this way, at the beginning of the 1990s, Rastafari culture arrived in Mexico City through the medium and influence of reggae music. This generated some misconceptions about Rastafari, because some people thought that Rastafari was exclusive to black people since this culture was born out of the traditions of the descendants of Africans who had been enslaved in the Americas and, therefore, each culture had to do with its history and roots according to their nationality and origin.

Additionally, in the early 1990s, it was not easy to access reggae music and it could not be found in any music stores or, if it was, it was expensive. This led to the creation of specialized points of informal trade where audio cassettes and later compact discs and videos from various reggae bands were sold, and whose owners accumulated impressive collections of musical material. From collections like this, and with the great influence of the *sonideros*,[11] who previously held the turntables, records, amplifiers, loudspeakers and started playing recorded music at popular parties in Mexico City (Fisher 2014, 73). In the early 1990s, the owners of these collections of reggae began to organize parties in private homes that drew upon the spirit of Jamaican sound systems. These deejays formed a larger group, the Hermandad Rasta, which emerged in 1997 in Mexico, spreading reggae to different parts of the city and, in 2005, creating Cultural Roots, a reggae club that continued the tradition of the sound system. Moreover, as producer and deejay Selecter Joshua (Josué Gómez Montoya, interview with author, Mexico City, 31 July 2010) has mentioned, it should be noted that the sounds system usually found more spaces for play on the outskirts of the city because, somehow, it was in these locations that the sound system was more accessible economically. In the same way, images related to the Rastafari culture began to be incorporated into the invitations for reggae events and parties. Along with the great festivals that began to multiply inside and outside of Mexico City, informal commerce and parties have become the meeting places among the members of the reggae community in Mexico.

On the other hand, by the mid-1990s, bands such as Ganja and La Comuna (in Mexico City) and La Yaga, El Cerco and El Mito (in Guadalajara), and I & I (in Yucatan) began to appear following the path of the Razteca bands. And by the end of that decade more bands appeared, like La Casa de Todos, La Reggata and Ghettos Band, among others, in different parts of the country that, in addition to the influence of roots reggae, also incorporated elements of dancehall and lovers'-rock reggae.

In 1996, the radio programme *Reggaeneracion* began on Orbita 105.7

THE DEVELOPMENT OF REGGAE MUSIC IN MEXICO

FM providing an option to include and spread the songs of Mexican reggae bands that already had their first album and creating a positive impact on the Mexican reggae scene of those years. In 2004, the programme became *Reggaevolucion* on Reactor 105.7 FM. It has been hosted since the beginning by Gerardo Pimentel "Zopi", vocalist and bassist of the band Rastrillos. This radio programme has specialized in various expressions of reggae music and until today has been characterized by including Mexican reggae in its programming. The show continues to air to date and has become an obligatory reference point for activities around reggae in Mexico City and interviews with international reggae personalities who frequently tour the country and perform in the city.

Third Period (2000–2009)

At the beginning of the twenty-first century, reggae music was expressed in different ways through different styles of reggae in Mexico. Technological developments such as the internet (and access to it) allowed for the emergence of new ways of making music that diluted the boundaries between musicians and deejays, allowing free vocals on electronic patterns or riddims that take place – for example, in the ragamuffin style – that allows one to create and act independently of a band. Around that same period, the Vibraciones de América Festival, which aimed to recreate the landscape of the reggae scene in Latin America, was started. There was also a revival of ska and early reggae in 2001 by skinheads and Mexican rudeboys via the band Jamaica 69, which distinguished itself from the Mexican bands of ska's third wave which had been popular in Mexico in the mid-1990s. Likewise, since 2002, a dub scene emerged in Mexico with the performances of Mad Professor and Lee "Scratch" Perry and bands like Bungalo Dub, Unidub Estación and Los Guanábana. Additionally, another wave of bands arose, like Victoria Malawi, Nognes, Kushia Bonton (in Mexico City), Los Atletas Campesinos (in Querétaro), Aire Nuevo (in Chiapas), Hierba Santa and CorpusKlan (in Chetumal), among many other new Mexican reggae bands with a strong influence from Latin American reggae bands like Los Pericos (1986), Gondwana (1987), Los Cafres (1987) and Cultura Profética (1996), from Argentina, Chile and Puerto Rico.

At the same time, Rastafari culture began to be assimilated differently by new generations. Since 2000, the lyrics of the Rasta singers or singers who spoke about Rastafari began to have a lot of impact on young people, and this gave rise to a sector of people eager to receive this information. The insertion of Mexico into the Latin American reggae network, as a result of Razteca Festival, facilitated the spread of information about the Rastafari movement in Spanish. By 2001, with the visit of the Chilean band Gondwana during the promotion tour of their album *Alabanza* (2000), a greater understanding of Rastafari was gained, based on the reasonings that some young Mexican Rastafari shared with Ras Don "Don Chico" (Dago Pérez), then-percussionist of the band and the most involved in the Rastafari faith, who explained that to be Rastafari one did not have to necessarily be black, speak English or forget one's roots. This band is considered the most important reggae band in Chile and, since its formation in 1987, cultivates and disseminates Rastafari culture through the lyrics of their songs. Therefore, Ras Don and, shortly after, the Afro-Argentinian musicians Fidel Nadal and Pablo Molina (former members of Todos Tus Muertos and Lumumba) are considered to be the first reggae musicians from Latin America more engaged in Rastafari understanding and faith, and their influence has contributed to a better understanding of Rastafari in Mexico. On his first visit, Ras Don shared important documentation that aided with the first meditations about Rastafari in Mexico. This generated great motivation among the young Rastafari and initiated a process of distinguishing the musical aspects, like reggae, from the spiritual ones, and establishing later contact with people who were involved in the Rastafari movement, like the Cuban Sister Lily in England. In 2004, Ras Don visited Mexico City for the third time and studied the statutes of the Nyahbinghi Order. Subsequently, the first Rastafari celebration was held on 2 November 2004 and a document was generated for *Rastafari Speak* magazine. This was the first document made by the Rastafari community in Mexico. The examples of Rastafari organizations in countries such as Chile and Panama have been of great importance to the development of Rastafari in Mexico. However, the lack of elders or representatives of the different Rastafari Orders[12] has caused the development of Rasta in Mexico, as well as the knowledge of its liturgy, to be slow because learning about it has often been through the information available on the Internet, which is mostly in English. However, since the Royal Visit Rastafari Chile in 2006 (when Jamaican Rastafari visited Chile), and subsequent expeditions to Peru, Ecuador and Colombia in 2008, more information became available in Spanish.

Thus, different Rastafari organizations emerged in Mexico City, where members meet to conduct studies and meditations on Rastafari culture, smoke ganja, share their mutual experiences and revelation, and begin to define themselves as members of a particular Rastafari Order. Consequently, Mexican Rastafari were present at the First Rastafari Summit of the Diaspora in the Hispanic World, held in Panama in May 2005, as well as at the Inaugural Conference of Rastafari Studies at the University of the West Indies in August 2010 and at the Second Rastafari Conference in August 2013, both held in Kingston, Jamaica. Mexican Rastafari also participated in "Ras Tafari: The Majesty and The Movement Exhibition" held in Addis Ababa, Ethiopia, in May 2014.

Based on the foregoing developments in Mexican Rastafari, since 2002 there also developed a form of reggae with Rastafari lyrics that spoke about Haile Selassie I, Jah, Zion, Babylon and other Rastafari concepts, done by singers or singjays like Ras Levy, Rebeleón, El Aarón and Rey León. These singers or singjays usually performed accompanied by a deejay, and displayed strong influences from conscious reggae and musicians like Capleton, Sizzla and Fidel Nadal, among others. Several of these musicians participated in the 2005 album *En el Juego del Dub*, which was the first work of the Mad Professor produced in Mexico. On the other hand, since 2003 the Rastreando el Reggae forum, organized by students of anthropology, emerged as the first space to address different aspects of reggae music and the Rastafari movement from an academic perspective.

In the second half of the 2000s there appeared a form of reggae with a stronger strain of social protest in its lyrics, alluding to different social problems that exist in the country and which was closer to ragga and hip-hop reggae. This form was usually accompanied only by a deejay and featured singers such as Lengualerta or Real Stylo among others. Finally, we must mention the emergence of a Christian reggae, following the style of bands like Christafari, presented by bands like Fuego Ardiente, led by former lead singer of Antidoping, Pepe Grela.

Fourth Period (2010 to present)

In the current period, reggae music continues to be expressed in different ways through the inclusion of different reggae styles in Mexico. In the early 2010s, there began to emerge a dancehall scene in Mexico with musicians like Roy Rebelde and Iman Souljah. It featured lyrics that spoke about the streets, the dance floor, or with sexual references that mimicked the current Jamaican dancehall and its slackness, with strong influences from musicians like Mad Cobra, Mavado, Mr Vegas, Turbulence and Vybz Kartel, among others. Furthermore, various groups such as Iniciativa Dancehall México and Pon Di Fyah have organized dancehall and twerking events and workshops. Although the development of dancehall in Mexico began in the 1990s with the deejays that included it as a musical subgenre of reggae music in the festivals and reggae clubs in Mexico City, later there emerged groups dedicated to dancehall music and soon after singers who began to interpret it in Spanish. In spite of being in search of a sound and its own identity, the dancehall that is produced in Mexico has been evolving through the efforts of promoters who produce major events, with dancers who have been trained in Jamaica and who host workshops when they return to Mexico as well as singers who have begun to leave the country to perform at major festivals, sign contracts with major labels and produce their own professional videos. In general, dancehall in Mexico is considered to be a part of the reggae scene as in Jamaica, but it is slowly gaining its own spaces, its own audience and its own place. However, sometimes dancehall is confused with reggaeton by those who do not know the musical genre well.

Almost simultaneously there arose a scene around electronic dance music and musical genres like drum and bass or dubstep with the Liga Mexicana del Bass, Sonido Berzerk or Alien's Dread following the style of bands like Digital Mystikz. At the same time, while there was this emergence of new representatives of existing styles, there also appeared new bands that retained the sound of the new roots, such as Sangre Maíz. Subsequently, another style of Rastafari reggae developed in Mexico with musicians like Leona de Etiopía, in the style of female singers like Queen Ifrica or Etana, presenting their own lyrics claiming Afro-Mexican roots. Furthermore, a nyahbinghi reggae that the Binghi Bongo Band performs incorporating the use of nyahbinghi drums, and with a direct influence from musicians like Count Ossie and the Mystic Revelation of Rastafari, Ras Michael and the Sons of Negus, and Inna de Yard, in addition to the Rastafari experience in Mexico of the last fifteen years. Interestingly, although this band had a short trajectory, it is the only Mexican reggae band that has performed at the Jamaican embassy in Mexico (along with the Black Star Band composed of Jamaican musicians who live in Mexico) because it incorporates traditional Rastafari music, that is to say nyahbinghi music, into its performances.

Conclusions

One can argue that, based on the song lyrics which speak of different issues, the designs of album covers, the predominant style, among many other performative aspects, we can identify different historical moments that relate to different styles of reggae but which, all together, comprise the development of reggae in Mexico.

The importance of reggae music in Mexico is unquestionable because since its adoption and subsequent adaptation, an important movement around this genre has been generated that, over time, has diversified itself. It is also important to note that although the release of an album or the initiation of a festival helps to distinguish one period from another, in general, the

FIGURE 3.3. Album: *Razteca: Sinergia Razteca en Movimiento*; artist: Various; year: 2000

FIGURE 3.4. Album: *Reggae Mexicano*; artist: Ganja; year: 2000.

dates are approximate and one cannot be too strict about the beginning or end of a period. As mentioned in the foregoing, these periods of reggae in Mexico actually show a continuum that has been expressed in a variety of ways and styles. Therefore, from the periodization that I have outlined, more research and analysis may be done to deepen each of these moments or perhaps to subdivide them where necessary. Nonetheless, the development of a periodization of this continuum is a useful mechanism through which to contextualize the development of this genre in Mexico at different times and to observe the characteristics of each stage or period. This also assists in the identification of changes or continuities between periods, or the assessment of similarities and differences in the development of reggae in Mexico with other Latin American countries, or even Jamaica. It should also be noted that emergence of a new period does not necessarily mean the disappearance of the former. Rather, it is more commonly found that different periods co-exist simultaneously, with musicians and bands representing each period, generating a particular expression, which, in turn, has different features and characteristics of the different styles of reggae music. This is similar to what happened in Jamaica when reggae emerged and rocksteady did not disappear, or when ska did not disappear upon the emergence of rocksteady. Today, bands like the Skatalites or musicians like Ken Boothe or Jimmy Cliff continue performing in their original style, even with the emergence of new bands and new artistes for the new forms of music.

In the case of Mexico, at festivals and spaces for reggae, bands that emerged in different periods and with different styles coexist. The most experienced bands that emerged in the second period of the development of reggae in Mexico and are currently still active, such as Rastrillos or Antidoping, are regarded as the leading bands of Mexican reggae. In addition to drawing large audiences, these bands often play with international reggae stars, go on tours, and participate in festivals in countries like the United States and Canada. Thus, the various bands, musicians, deejays, singjays and sound systems that make up the reggae scene in Mexico currently coexist in the same period and, in some cases, have begun to interact and collaborate not only among themselves but also with international musicians. However, many times, the reggae audience in Mexico may be more willing to pay for a ticket to a concert showcasing a foreign reggae band instead of for one to a concert showcasing a Mexican band.

Ultimately, although reggae music has been present in Mexico since the 1970s and major festivals are held annually, the few academic works that address the international reggae scene do not include the reggae scene in Mexico specifically.[13] Nonetheless, this scene has continued to gain strength, not only through the work and career of Mexican reggae bands, or the inclusion, increasingly, of Mexico within the tours of the main and current exponents of reggae globally, but also through the inclusion of some new artists like Jah Fabio on major labels such as VP Records.

It is also important to mention some non-musical aspects that are part of the reggae scene in Mexico that give us an idea of how Mexicans perceive this genre, such as the participation of Mexican artists and designers who have achieved significant recognition in the International Reggae Poster Contest, an initiative designed to celebrate positive international reggae culture highlighting the globalization of reggae and the resounding impact of its message.[14] Graphic designer and illustrator Maria Papaefstathiou (interview with author, 17 February 2017), co-founder of the contest, comments that folk arts, religion and family permeate almost everything in modern Mexico, so much that even its graphic design culture is deeply rooted in native heritage and traditions. This influence is reflected in the motifs, hand-drawn or textured elements, bold and bright colours, and intricate details of the posters entered. Another reason that Mexican designers participate is their love for the country and the music. Some winners are shown in figure 3.5.

Based on my research to date, I consider that when the next period emerges, the fifth reggae period in Mexico, some elements will be present. For example, there will probably be more interaction between the different actors who make up the reggae scene in this country, such as bands, musicians and singers collaborating with deejays in the creation of their own songs, as well as deejays including Mexican reggae songs as part of their set at reggae parties and clubs; greater development in the musical and lyrical quality of the musicians of each genre and style; greater development of the local bands of different states of the country; greater media presence through professional music videos; and a greater inclusion on the radio and television. Similarly, it is probable that more reggae songs will emerge in some Mexican indigenous

FIGURE 3.5. Mexican winners of the International Reggae Poster Contest

languages or incorporating different traditional musical instruments and fusing some traditional Mexican music in different parts of the country.

Certainly, there will also be more attempts by the mainstream to appropriate this music, trying to merge it with genres as the *banda*, especially in the subgenres of *norteño-banda* and *corridos*, as the case of the singer Gerardo Ortiz, who sings Bob Marley's "Is This Love" in this style. However, the reggae scene in Mexico still needs to strengthen several aspects that will allow for further consolidation of this scene at the local, regional and national levels, and thereby generate greater international dissemination. Knowledge of the development of the story allows us to explain what reggae music brings to Mexican musical cultures, and what could be Mexico's contribution to global reggae music. This work is a step in this direction.

Notes

1. The Mexican Caribbean refers to a geographic zone that includes the coastline of the Yucatan Peninsula, continuing along the Caribbean coast of Quintana Roo.
2. The *jarana jarocha* is a guitar-shaped fretted stringed instrument from the southern region of the State of Veracruz, Mexico. It is played in the traditional music of the region, carved from a single piece of wood; it usually has eight strings in five courses (the double strings in the middle). The jarana is played percussively with up and down strokes and is assigned the number 321.322-5 in the Hornbostel-Sachs classification of musical instruments.
3. Tropical music is a generic term used to refer to the several variants of music generated from the nineteenth century in the area surrounding the Caribbean Sea and the Caribbean region of the American continent and encompassing various musical genres such as salsa, cumbia, bachata, merengue and vallenato, among others.
4. *Discotheque Orfeon a Go-gó* was a musical television show for Mexican youth and the first dedicated to spreading youth music in Spanish in Mexico, including rock 'n' roll. It was broadcast in Mexico from 1961 to 1969.
5. Since 1970, in order to encourage migration to the border town of Chetumal, a federation-led colonization process has begun to repopulate and recover areas on the border of Mexico with British Honduras (now Belize) and towards the Caribbean coast. The project, directed to the border area delimited by the

Hondo River, consisted of an ambitious settlement plan that had as its centre an agro-industrial riparian project.

6. The *Festival Rock y Ruedas de Avándaro* (also known as the *Festival de Avándaro*) was a historic Mexican rock concert held on 11–12 September 1971, on the shores of Lake Avándaro in the central state of Mexico. The festival took place at the height of La Onda (a multidisciplinary artistic movement created in Mexico by artists and intellectuals as part of the world-wide waves of the counterculture of the 1960s, its followers were called *onderos, macizos* or *jipitecas*) and celebrated life, youth, ecology, music, peace and free love. This milestone in the history of Mexican rock music has been compared to the Woodstock Festival held in New York in 1969 for its psychedelic music, counterculture imagery and artwork, and open drug use.

7. Because of the repression of rock music by the Mexican government after the massive Avándaro Festival, in subsequent years the concerts were held almost exclusively on *hoyos fonquis* (funky holes), which were dilapidated houses, abandoned factories, crumbling cinemas or theatres. In these spaces, the bands played at ground level and often were not paid, but by then they were the only venues for the bands and the only places where you could hear rock made in Mexico.

8. *Rock en tu Idioma* (Rock in your Language) was an outreach campaign, promoted and produced by the record company BMG Ariola, to publicize and distribute bands of Mexican, Spanish and Argentine rock and incorporating other record labels. The campaign went on from 1986 to 1990.

9. The name *Razteca* suggests the idea of a fusion of the Rastafarian root of reggae music with the Mexican Aztec root, and also alluding to the *jipitecas* (hippie/Aztec) of the 1970s.

10. The Zapatista Army of National Liberation is a revolutionary group in Chiapas in southern Mexico. It fights against neoliberalism and for self-determination by the local indigenous peoples. This movement aligns itself with the wider alter-globalization, anti-neoliberal social movement, seeking indigenous control over their local resources, especially land.

11. *Sonidero* is a term used in Mexico to designate the owner of audio, animator and programmer of popular music, performing dance events both outdoors and indoors in popular areas of the city. It should be noted that the *sonidero* deejay specializes in tropical music. There is no concrete data about which *sonidero* began this practice, but a pair of neighbourhoods of Mexico City would be were precursors to this phenomenon during the 1960s: Tepito and Peñón de los Baños.

12. Rastafarian Orders are ramifications of the same movement. These include the

THE DEVELOPMENT OF REGGAE MUSIC IN MEXICO

    Bobo Ashanti (Ethiopia Africa Black International Congress), the Nyahbinghi (Theocracy Reign Ivine Order of the Nyahbinghi), the Twelve Tribes of Israel and others. Frequently referred to as Mansions, the term is taken from the biblical verse John 14:2.

13. See Davis and Simon (1983), Alleyne and Dunbar (2012), Cooper (2012), and Hope (2013, 2015).
14. The International Reggae Poster Contest was founded by Michael Thompson and Maria Papaefstathiou in 2011. The umbrella term "reggae," as used by the organizers, encompasses all the popular Jamaican musical genres: ska, rocksteady, roots reggae, dub, dancehall and the unique Jamaican sound system. Outlined below are the names of the Mexicans who have been selected in the International Reggae Poster Contest and the place they got in each competition, in its first four editions (see http://www.reggaepostercontest.com/gallery/).

2012
12 – Sergio Ortiz Aguilar
19 – Gamma Jam Jam
52 – Edmundo – Galindo
59 – Gamma Jam Jam
60 – Iván Fuentes
63 – Oscar Ramírez
68 – Freddy Peralta
100 – Alexis Tapia

2013
3 – Lenin Baru Vásquez Felipe
20 – Nancy Reyes
46 – Alexi Jacobo – Vidal Romero
66 – Erika Bonilla Bouchan
76 – Alexis Tapia
81 – José Alberto Torres Pérez

2014
5 – Luis Daniel Pérez Molina
19 – Cristian Cedillo Rodríguez
91 – Alexis Tapia
94 – Alexis Barrios

2015
5 – Diego Parra
10 – Octavio López
23 – Martin Navarro
31 – Ricardo Vázquez

51 – Luis García
77 – Moisés Romero
80 – Daniela Alvarado
2016
44 – Martin Navarro

References

Alleyne, Mike, and Sly Dunbar. 2012. *The Encyclopedia of Reggae: The Golden Age of Roots Reggae*. New York: Sterling.
Benavente, Carolina. 2005. *¿Dónde está el toque Jamaiquino? reggae y Rasta-reggae en México, D.F.* Buenos Aires: Actas del VI Congreso de la Rama Latinoamericana de la Asociación Internacional para el Estudio de la Música Popular.
Bennett, Andy, and Richard A. Peterson, eds. 1994. *Music Scenes: Local, Translocal and Virtual*. Nashville, TN: Vanderbilt University Press.
Cohen, Sara. 1999. "Scenes". In *Key Terms in Popular Music and Culture,* edited by Bruce Horner and Thomas Swiss, 239–50. Oxford: Blackwell, 1999.
Connell, John, and Chris Gibson. 2001. *Sound Tracks: Popular Music, Identity and Place*. London: Routledge.
Cooper, Carolyn, ed. *Global Reggae*. Jamaica: University of the West Indies Press, 2012.
Davis, Stephen, and Peter Simon. 1983. *Reggae International*. New York: R & B.
Enríquez Montes, Florencio Arturo. 2014. *Reggae en el Caribe Mexicano*, Mexico City: Asociación Editorial Alebrijez
Fernández Monte, Gonzalo Javier. 2012. "El ska en España: escena alternativa, musical y trasnacional". PhD dissertation, Universidad Complutense de Madrid.
Fisher, Jonathan. 2014. "Sonidero City: Sound Systems in Mexiko". *Riddim Magazine* 2 (March/April): 73.
Hope, Donna P., ed. 2013. *International Reggae*. Kingston, Jamaica: Pelican Publishers.
———. 2015. *Reggae from Yaad*, Kingston, Jamaica: Ian Randle.
López-Negrete Miranda, Christian Eugenio. 2013. "El reggae que llegó a México". In *Una nota de reggae,* edited by Cristian Cedillo, Adrián Jorge and Edgardo Rosales, 10–15. Mexico City: UACM/ACE Colectivo.

CHAPTER 4

PETER TOSH, SOCIAL PROTEST AND JAMAICAN CURSE WORDS

RACQUEL BERNARD

Civil Rights activist and freedom singer Bernice Johnson Reagon speaks to the importance of music to communicate where the silenced and marginalized cannot. Her experience in the Civil Rights Movement of the United States showed her that songs can defy social structures: "As a singer and activist in the Albany Movement, I sang and heard the freedom songs, and saw them pull together sections of the Black community at times when other means of communication were ineffective. It was the first time that I knew the power of song to be an instrument for the articulation of our community concerns" (Smithsonian Folkways 2003). In the particular context of freedom songs, part of their power came from their participatory and communal nature. Song bound protestors together. The song of the movement, "We Shall Overcome", required a mirroring of its message of unity with a physical sign of crossing the forearms then holding hands to bring people closer together. Even in the absence of collective action social movements, music is a powerful mode of social critique. During the same era of the Civil Rights movement, emerging reggae takes on similar functions as freedom songs. The genre is often framed as conscious music, although it has always included subject matter related to all realms of life. Reggae has largely been associated with social commentary and protest. In this chapter, I elucidate the dimensions of one reggae artist who epitomized the freedom-fighting lens of reggae.

Peter Tosh produced music from the mid-1960s until the late 1980s. His work addressed police brutality, classicism, colourism, anti-apartheid protest, unreliable friends, glorifying Jah, sex and more. His explicitly political lyrics captured frustration with an era in Jamaica that was rocked by alarming socio-economic conditions for the majority of Jamaicans. Tosh expounded a vision of pan-African uplift with his music and words. Positioning himself as a representative of and voice for poor and underprivileged people in Jamaica, he rarely refused the opportunity to speak his own truth and prophesy the downfall of the neocolonial *shitstem*.[1]

I introduce Tosh as a black radical prophet and as an artist speaking back at black inferiority. I first conceptualize Tosh as speaking against white and brown bias in Jamaican society, and frame him as a reggae revolutionary whose cosmology is influenced by Rastafari and a number of other ideologies about black consciousness in the 1960s and 1970s. Following this, I focus on his use of Jamaican curse words in songs, onstage "livatribes",[2] and daily life. Language drives my argument as I place Tosh's use of these expletives within the postcolonial structures that align standard English with power and social capital as opposed to Jamaican Patois or Creole, which is seen as informal and indicating lack of formal education. Before further discussion of Tosh's work, I present a brief biographical sketch and an overview of the sociopolitical landscape of Jamaica during his era.

Peter Tosh was born Winston Hubert McIntosh on 19 October 1944 in Westmoreland, Jamaica. During his childhood, his mother was not his primary caregiver and he had little contact with his father. In his earliest years, he showed a keen affinity for music. He began to sing at two years old. At five, he made his own instrument and would collect shillings for singing and playing. He grew up with his aunt and other family members (Tulloch 2013, 4).

Their household was Christian, specifically Pentecostal. He would sing in church and at school. Tosh "became distracted", left high school early and moved to Kingston when he was seventeen. The first trade he pursued in his new urban home was welding, but he would soon focus most of his energy on creating music. He continued to develop his musical craft alongside his bandmates Bob Marley and Bunny Livingston (later Bunny Wailer). Under the mentorship of Joe Higgs, the Wailers found their sound and name (Masouri 2013, 29). In 1963, Peter, Bob, Bunny and a new addition to the group, Beverly

Kelso, performed for Clement "Sir Coxsone" Dodd, a popular deejay who began recording one-off acetate discs (dub plates) five years earlier (30). Tosh recorded two singles on Dodd's Studio One label "The Toughest" and "Shame and Scandal" (Tulloch 2013, 7).

In 1965, Coxsone signed a distribution deal with the label Island Records, owned by white Jamaican Chris Blackwell (Masouri 2013, 41). As the business relationship continued, Peter and Bunny would clash with Coxsone over money (50). For example, Peter Tosh rewrote "Sinner Man" as "Downpressor Man" and had been singing it for years, yet "Coxsone credited the 45 to 'Bob Marley and the Wailers', despite Bob having nothing to do with it" (46). Eventually, this configuration of the Wailers would split up and Bunny and Peter continued their music in the growing shadow of Bob. Peter Tosh's first solo album was *Legalize It* (1976). The song "Legalize It" advocated for the legalization of marijuana, enumerated its medicinal qualities and declared that individuals from all classes used it. It was an instant hit even though it was banned. His second album, *Equal Rights* (1977), went gold. After his split from the Wailers, Tosh's run-ins with the law became more frequent. He was brutalized by the police for marijuana possession (Campbel 1993).

Several friends and acquaintances characterize a final chapter of Peter Tosh's life that was marked by increased anxiety, suspicion and a loss of his firm self-assurance. In the film *Steppin' Razor: Red X* (Campbel 1993), some interviewees associate this change with his relationship with Marlene Brown. Evah Gordon explains, "We start to see a different Peter now. You start to see the duppy part of Peter now . . . she awoke this duppy part." I caution that these assumptions are cinematically employed as a narrative device to frame Tosh's death. One should compare these representations to more sympathetic instances, such as Marlene Brown's account in the Los Angeles–based magazine *Reggae and African Beat*. Brown reports that she sensed that something was wrong in the months before Tosh's murder. In the preceding weeks she "felt death" in the house and warned him (Aylmer 1987, 22). He died tragically on 11 September 1987. His home was invaded by his "friend" Dennis "Leppo" Lobban and two other men. They shot and killed him, Wilton "Doc" Brown and Jeff "Free I" Dixon and wounded three others. Leppo was sentenced to prison; the two other men have never been found or tried. As with a number of revolutionary voices of this time, the circumstances of his death are highly disputed. After his death, he was awarded a Grammy for his album *No Nuclear War*.

Jamaica during Tosh's Era

During the mid-1960s, the Jamaica Labour Party failed to fulfil campaign promises for economic improvement and stability. Thinkers such as Walter Rodney, a Guyanese-born lecturer at the University of the West Indies, were espousing ideas of Black Power, shifting access to history towards the poor and partnering with once predominantly politically withdrawn Rastafarians. By this time, "a visiting US sociological team could conclude that 'Jamaica had the highest rate of income inequality in the world'" (Mills 2010, 103). Jamaica and its cultural output were contributing to global conversations about race, class and power. Kamau Brathwaite, Barbadian poet and historian, describes 1966–67 as a defining moment when Stokely Carmichael visited London. He observes (2004, 510): "From London (and Black America) the flame spread to the university campuses of the archipelago. It found echoes among the urban restless of the growing island cities. Rastafari art, 'primitive' art, dialect and protest verse suddenly had a new urgency, took on significance."

Walter Rodney often called for black people in Jamaica to be more in control of their destinies and regarded the teaching of African history as a productive force. This elevation of black history interacts with what Deborah Weeks (2008, 31) notes as a central premise to Black Power in Richard Newman's work *Black Power and Black Religion* "that before black people can obtain some of the power and wealth that they had helped to create, they must learn to love and respect themselves" (Weeks 2008, 31).

While groups like Rastafari remained as loci of black consciousness in Jamaica, the initial post-independence period was marked by political anxiety around a cultural focus on African heritage. This anxiety emerges from various historical moments. For example, Deborah Thomas (2004, 71) cites the 1960 Henry Rebellion, a pre-independence revolt that sought to defy both colonial governance and the impending nationalist government in order to establish a black government.[3] Stephen A. King (2002, 47) points out an important irony concerning Jamaica's relationship with an increasingly imperial United States in the era following independence, saying, "although increasingly tied to the US economy, the Jamaican government clearly disapproved of one import from the mainland: radical black nationalism". Walter Rodney's work in this cultural context is a nuanced threat to conservative Jamaican government. Thomas (2004, 76) argues that Rodney's "expulsion by the Jamaican government spoke to a fear on the part of the [Jamaica Labour Party] that forging links between university intellectuals and grassroots leaders could result in radical political mobilization powerful enough to threaten the young state".

While the Jamaican government argued that Rodney's support of the Black Power movement was anti-Jamaican because it contradicted the ideal of a multicultural Jamaica, the same officials upheld colonial structures, using colonial law against people labelled subversive (Ledgister 2008, 80).[4] The Jamaican government chose to ban Rodney from the country and from lecturing at the University of the West indies in 1968. In response to the ban, lecturers and students at the university organized a peaceful meeting which transformed into a full-blown riot.[5]

After Black Power's short, but explosive, articulation in Jamaica, socioeconomic conditions did not improve. The intensity of political violence rose to alarming levels and events such as the Green Bay Massacre[6] exemplified the depth of corruption and turmoil. Charles Mills explains that by the late 1960s unemployment rates were well over 20 per cent and would have been higher without massive migration to Britain first, then North America (Mills 2010, 103).

It is within this context that Peter Tosh's personality, often perceived as "overly aggressive and alienating, even to admirers", must be placed (Davies 2000, 3). As an artist, Tosh faced several setbacks, within and outside of his control, but maintained a staunch faith in himself, his outlook and his calling. He did not receive mass approval for his work by Jamaicans, due in part to "his liberal use of Jamaican curse words and his open advocacy of the legitimization of ganja [which] did not endear him to the authorities or to the Jamaican middle class" (3).

Tosh understood his fate as one linked to that of black people everywhere, which allowed him to expose a full system of racial *downpression* through his music. Tosh had an "uncompromising and sustained anti-apartheid stance, beginning with the Equal Rights album [which] has no equal in reggae, or pop music for that matter" (Davies 2000, 7). His early condemnation of the system is impressive as apartheid became a particularly urgent topic for activism and music.

1960s–1980s Black Radicalism in the Caribbean

The 1960s–1980s was a period marked by the widespread circulation of ideas, art and social movements around black racial uplift. This period included protests and other cultural output associated with the US Civil Rights Movement, Black Power, francophone African and Caribbean Negritude, Jamaican Rastafari and the anti-apartheid South African Black Consciousness Movement. Black consciousness, as categorical shorthand, had global iterations that complicated notions of what blackness meant. For various nations in the Caribbean, Black Power as articulated in the United States was no simple stamp for local identity politics. Some Caribbean governments responded by restricting activists from crossing international borders. Stokley Carmichael, a Trinidadian-born activist who led in the Student Non-violent Coordinating Committee and the Black Panther Party, was not allowed to enter Jamaica. Notions of black racial uplift from the United States also met resistance because of the position of Caribbean nations within the global and local economy. For some, Carmichael's philosophy was perceived as having no place in Trinidad due to the nation's location in a racially integrated society which needed good relations with white people to continue economically (Lowenthal 1972, 129).

David Lowenthal explains that unlike the United States, Caribbean blacks in high positions were seen as a part of the exploitative postcolonial system (129). Some US-oriented blacks, such as Martin Luther King Jr and Stokely Carmichael, assumed that black visibility in government positions and other respected occupations in the Caribbean indicated relative racial harmony. However, the black people in these positions usually give self-preservation precedence over solidarity with other black people. In order to elucidate this point, Lowenthal states that, in Haiti, Black Power is already state power (129). In a 1969 publication, René Despestre (2004, 244) argues that "those black and mulatto bourgeoisie have perfected the mechanisms of oppression and the alienating networks inherited from the colonial system and cause to fall back on them, all the barbarism which in the courses of the last centuries, dehumanized the history of the peoples of the Third World". Whereas black communities in the United States faced legal segregation from whites, these poor black communities faced a valorization of European colonial values by an often predominantly coloured middle class. Lowenthal (1972, 126) explains that Black Power fused with a largely West Indian movement: negritude. Despestre (2004, 242) describes negritude and its opposition to "negrismo": a European acknowledgement of African influence in West Indian society that relied on stereotypes. In thinking of the difference between the two, Despestre (242) says "there exists every qualitative difference that exists between an ordinary wick and the wick of a dynamite". Negritude seeks to destroy stereotypes and to advocate for those who must claim themselves in a society that depicts them as Zombis (243).

As in the case of Negritude, ideas such as Black Power met local articulations of social critique in Jamaica. Rex Nettleford describes Rastafari in Jamaica as a force that questioned "the society's identity in terms of its racial and cultural antecedents . . .[; they did so] on the basis of open confrontation which was to become the feature of protest everywhere in the sixties" (Despestre 2004, 127).

David Lowenthal (1972, 127) argues that "Black Power in the Caribbean is anticolored as well as antiwhite". Although one can turn to the United States for analogous structures of white bias which allow lighter skinned African Americans to access other forms of social capital, Lowenthal (127) correctly asserts that "West Indian distinctions between black and mulatto had only limited relevance . . . to Negroes in the United States". The "one-drop" rule that legally inscribed blackness on any person with traceable African ancestry accommodates for solidarity regardless of shade. This accommodation, in spite of patterns of white bias in racial leadership and access to the intellectual class, is contested periodically. For example, Lowenthal (129) notes that Marcus Garvey's work in the United States after 1916 met wide approval by darker African Americans who felt ignored by the (often lighter skinned) intellectual leadership associated with W.E.B. Du Bois's notion of the "Talented Tenth". Despite such examples, identity based on shade and colour still necessitates more tenuous negotiation because of class structures within creolized Caribbean nations.

Lowenthal (1972, 129) argues that these racial identity differences mean that Black Power is unlikely to remain viable in the Caribbean, where a 1970 *Tapia* column described Trinidadians as revolting against "a black-skinned Afro-saxon administration". Those who were most emphatic about Black Power were usually light skinned, a position that makes them open to critiques of representing "the black masses" (129). For the large East Indian–descended populations in places like Trinidad, Guyana and Suriname, Black Power poses additional problems.

Jamaica within Global Black Radicalism

Peter Tosh's experiences expose some ways that official authorities within Jamaica work to quell black radical demonstration. Peter Tosh was involved in the riots which occurred after Walter Rodney's ban. He drove a bus into a store, people looted it and then he drove them back to Trench Town. Police officer Joe Williams learned of Tosh's involvement through the common practice of surveilling poor urban communities and, thereafter, monitored him closely (Masouri 2013, 66). Carter Mathes exposes a moment in which Jamaica is misunderstood as a nation of racial harmony in an analysis with Martin Luther King Jr's visit to Jamaica. Mathes reflected on the likely preferential treatment that King would have received during his visit which allowed him to look to Jamaica's national motto "Out of many, one people" and conclude that the Jamaican sociopolitical landscape was harmonious. This misreading is often promoted by the "concept of *creole multiracial nationalism,* an idea of a common cultural heritage as proof of the legitimacy of Jamaican independence within a global narrative of liberal progress, obscuring the realities of racial division while embracing folk cultural sensibilities as markers of the past from which modern Jamaicans had progressed" (Mathes 2010, 23). Mathes (19) notes that Jamaica enters the global state with a deep ambivalence about the degree to which blackness defined Jamaican identity. As a dark-skinned Jamaican, Tosh found little space for such indecision.

Anthony Bogues centralizes mainstream ambivalence when he begins one of his articles with the scene of a young man getting beaten by police for attending a "Black Power school" (Bogues 2009). Bouges centralizes these issues immediately: knowledge of black history as a threat to state power and the general use of force to curtail its progress. Charles Mills (2010, 104) argues that "white ruling-class fears about black militancy are in certain important ways not dissimilar psychologically from the earlier ubiquitous Great House dread of possible slave insurrection". Bogues (2009, 135) notes that Rastafari and Rodney threatened the government officials such as Prime Minister Shearer, who attempted to take rebellion out of the notion of Black Power and limit it to "dignity". In this framework, Tosh presents his response to state power and its systemic opposition against poor black people.

Although Black Power in Jamaica was often policed, directly following independence, Jamaican popular culture served as calls of black elevation that affected communities in Jamaica and the Caribbean diaspora. Literary poets and musical poets engaged in explosive ideology exchange. After reflecting on founding the Caribbean Artists Movement in *Timehri*, Kamau Brathwaite (2004, 511) speaks to the time when he was about to start publishing his "trilogy of long poems, influenced by those resurrectionary years in Ghana, and tightened by my contact with Jamaican society with its black consciousness and its controlled rage and implosive violence, the sound of ska, rock-steady, reggae, and Orlando Patterson's the *Children of Sisyphus* (1964)". Brathwaite exposes the ways that art forms such as literature and music influence each other. He sees Jamaican popular culture as instrumental to his own creative output. Peter Tosh's friends and acquaintances often mention his own avid reading habits as a central source of his understanding of black politics and an inspiration for his music. Thus, across nations, government agendas worked against Black Power while popular culture embraced and promoted it.

In Jamaica, class complicates and often silences black consciousness. Charles Mills (2010, 103) explains that Jamaica's class structure in the 1950s and 1960s corresponds closely with colour: "not one of the twenty-one families which dominating the economy was of African origin". Unlike many middle-class Jamaicans, Peter Tosh identified with the lower middle class, the poor, and embraced black politics. He had no problem showcasing his alliance when he wore the Black Power fist (Masouri 2013, 73). He expressed his alliance with resourcefulness and creativity. He carved Black Power pendants and made Afro combs (74–78). Because of his colour and class, Tosh does not have the option of creating a de-racialized fantasy of Jamaica as his middle-class counterparts do. The following section further unpacks the dimensions within Peter Tosh's observation "From I born, me learn say, 'If you're brown, you can stick around; if you're white then you perfectly alright and if you black, stay back'" (9–10). The following section provides an overview of the foundation of Jamaican race and colour identity politics by examining the nation within Caribbean creolization.

Jamaican Creolization and White Bias[7]

The legacies of slavery and colonialism are fundamental in understanding the process of Caribbean creolization. In current scholarship, the process incorporates several heritage claims. In *Caribbean Creolization* (1998), Kathleen M. Balutansky and Marie-Agnés Sourieau define créolité as "a syncretic process of transverse dynamics that endlessly reworks and transforms cultural patterns of varied social and historical experiences and identities" (quoted in Hintzen, 2002, 99). As populations with different ethnic backgrounds migrate to Caribbean spaces, the colour/class continuums of those societies modify. Percy Hintzen (99) identifies that "it is through racial and cultural incorporation that the transitory nature of Creole society is preserved".

Jamaica, a nation with a predominantly African-descended population, has a creolization process that starts in the nationalist era with a continued exaltation of whiteness. Hintzen (95) asserts that "whiteness, however tainted, retains its valorized position in Creole-nationalist construction". The process extends to the brown elite's articulation of multiracial and non-racial national ideals and exists amid a contestation for modern blackness. Rex Nettleford (2004, 473) characterizes Jamaica as a coloured nation obsessed with the multiracial image of themselves and as a nation of immigrants where no group can call themselves sons of the soil other than the mixed-race people born after colonialism began (given the unjust decimation of indigenous peoples). Nettleford (470) describes the social pyramid of society with whites at the apex, brown or mixed race at the centre, and blacks at the base. Valorizing whiteness and the accompanying obsession with "proximity to whiteness" is connected to the network of privileges associated with brownings (light-skinned black people). Donna Hope (2011, 167) explains that "the conflation of skin colour with power, a pervasive shadism, remains a social and cultural legacy of Jamaica's slavery and colonial history, with lighter skin (identified as 'brown' in Jamaica) still perceived as positive and ideal". As it relates to beauty aesthetics, "brownings are perceived as more desirable than their dark-skinned counterparts" (Brown-Glaude 2007, 40).

Michael Hanchard (2008, 60) explores the ways that Jamaica operates as a majority black nation that is more focused on localized regional identity markers than race and operates on a memory that ignores racial tensions. The existing valorization of European ancestry complicates debates on the proper deconstruction and use of the nation's motto, "Out of many, one people", particularly when in conversation with "modern blackness". Milton Vickerman asserts that the motto espoused by the brown elite after independence captures multiracialism and ironic non-racialism that imagined Jamaica as a "color-blind meritocracy" (Brown-Glaude 2007, 39). The motto projects an image of cohabitation and ironically centralizes the moment of miscegenation despite the African-descended population's clear majority over mixed populations. Even if one destabilizes the category of African heritage to acknowledge multiple regional and ethnic identities that give rise to the black majority, the ideology of the motto is undermined by clear economic and political structures that align colour and class. How can the "many" truly be "one" people if brown-skinned people are "over-represented among Jamaica's elite?" (40).

Reading Tosh as Black Radical Prophet

After listening to several of Tosh's interviews, one can recognize a certain kind of language and vocabulary that he launches against systems of oppression. He performs to some extent what Anthony Bogues (2003, 19) presents as "the language of prophecy". It is "poetic and visionary, and is rooted in conceptions of history". For example, while speaking about the systems that operate within the music industry to exploit singers and artists, Tosh inserts poetic claims: "I don't want to be a superstar, I am not a star. I was born, SUN, and the sun ever shine" (Abbott 2012a). When Tosh speaks about His Imperial Majesty Haile Selassie I, he exemplifies language for the black radical political tradition: "this language is embedded in two sources, biblical exegesis and the indigenous knowledge systems of the colonized native" (Bogues 2003, 19). Tosh often speaks with biblical verses while divorcing the notion of the Christian God for Jah, who is the accurate divine father for Tosh.

In Tosh's prophetic Red X tapes, he deconstructs Jamaican postcolonial society while elucidating the ignored images of working-class, poor, Rastafari under state apparatus. I examine the prophetic themes within Tosh's work and further interrogate him as a participant in a wider black consciousness radical tradition. Omar Davies (2000, 3) points to these themes, stating that "his strident and consistent anti-apartheid stance [came] long before the cause of Mandela made it a popular position to take". He "tackled head-on the issues of apartheid, nuclear war, police brutality, politics, poverty, and racism with a vengeance" (Tulloch 2013, xv).

I frame a prophet as someone who criticizes the corrupt practices of a government or society and sends/records the messages. To refer to himself, Tosh preferred the title preacher over reggae superstar or entertainer (oravcik 2011).[8] When asked if he sees himself a prophet, he responded that he sees himself as a preacher concerned with sending messages (ND 2011). I analyse Tosh's cultural legacy while asserting that preaching and prophetic experience allow supernatural transformation and transition. The vision outlives the prophet. Tosh did not simply speak prophetically, but also bore bodily shame. The police brutality and oppression Tosh faced are reminders of similar assaults on lower-middle-class Jamaicans that have not been recorded in the same way.

Taitu Heron and Yanique Hume (2012, 36) have explored Peter Tosh's "interpretation of Afro-Christianity in Rastafari [which] declares his faith, convictions and belief in the fulfilment of the scriptures in many of his songs". It is important to keep in mind that his songs against societal injustice are linked to the bodily harassment he undergoes again and again. Heron and Hume (41) explain, "His profile as dark-skinned, working class black makes him more vulnerable to the forces of injustice." At the core of tensions around injustice is the ideology gap between those suffering from injustice and those who benefit from it. Beneficiaries do not recognize their own privileges and rest on assumptions that the oppressed have an illogical work ethic. Peter Tosh speaks against a social structure that applauds and envies the wealth of the small elite without scrutinizing the sustained legacies of plantation slavery.

Tosh Speaking Back at Black Inferiority

Heron and Hume (2012, 26) position Peter Tosh's work in a "tradition of resistance, which has sought to reclaim and rehabilitate the dignity of blackness and to redress societal imbalances". The construction of the Caribbean as a singularized slave society brought with it the diffusion of what Gordon K. Lewis calls "a virulent negrophobia", which promoted the idea that enslaved Africans were inferior to their European masters. This negrophobia led to oppressive practices, material and symbolic, by the hegemonic European-identified groups (Balsini 2009, 75–76). To better frame the dimensions of black inferiority that Tosh strives against, I turn to an overview of Rastafari and its influence on reggae music.

Rastafari and Reggae

Speaking about the Wailers' transition into Rastafari (catalysed by Rita Marley's brother), Roger Steffens points out: "They start saying 'Rastafari' and making wild talk. . . . Bob start to grow his hair, Peter start and Bunny not combing his hair any more either . . . they pass their spliff to me and I back away from it, because I did not want no part of that" (Masouri 2013, 44). One can perceive the scepticism and belittling of Rastafari in Steffen's words. Since the 1930s through much of the post-independence era, Rastafari was understood as deviant and worthy of contempt. Bongo Israel, a Nyabinghi elder, explains that police officers would seize them in the streets and cut off their locks (Campbel 1993). Unlike the current era in which Rastafari has been incorporated into mainstream Jamaican popular culture, Rastafari first operated as a subculture[9] beginning in the 1930s and then shifted to a counterculture around 1960s and 1970s. Rastafari, which was first loosely organized and without distinct leaders, had transitioned into an organized counterculture with leaders and clear ideas during Peter Tosh's years of artistry.

In order to frame Peter Tosh's response to anti-black rhetoric and systems, I emphasize Heron and Hume's use of Rastafari as a theology of liberation

(2012, 28). They explain that two important sites in Rastafari ideology are Babylon and Africa. The biblical city Babylon, where captured Jews were enslaved, became reconfigured and reinterpreted as parallel to African existence in the Caribbean (28). This reinterpretation begins with a comparison of the enslavement of African people and their descendants in the Caribbean and grows to include institutions and persons associated with modern capitalism and its relations of domination: the slave master, the head driver, the colonial officer, the missionary, the church, the pope, European colonial powers and British monarchs (28).

In post-independence Jamaican society, "Babylon" begins to refer to various neocolonial situations – that is, excessive brutality in the police force, familial favouritism and corruption in government, and the often oligarchic nature of the private sector (28). Unlike Babylon, Africa is understood as a realm of freedom and dignity (29). Heron and Hume characterize Rastafari as having Protestant ethic with central ideologies of Ethiopia as essential African heritage and Zionism (32). Rastafari relies on a biblical source but interprets with a liberatory perspective (32).

Reggae's birth in 1968 "signalled the beginning of a wholesale embrace of the Rastafarian faith and more radical political themes in Jamaican popular music" (King 2002, 46). According to Stephen King, reggae became more explicitly political and "A whole generation began to wear dreadlocks . . . to talk about Ethiopia and Mount Zion" (46). Reggae can be defined as a choppy syncopated groove built around an organ shuffle and rhythm guitar (Masouri 2013, 72). In the transition from rocksteady to reggae, vague Rastafarian promises of repatriation and unification shifted to specific singing about concepts such as "Jah", "Babylon" and "Mount Zion" (King 2002, 47). Stephen King, P. Foster and Barry T. Bays note that reggae was distinguished by its use of Jamaican patois and increasingly more explicit tool for protest (King 2002, 46).

Through the reclamation of black heritage via Rastafari and the empowering genre of social critique that reggae was becoming, Tosh advocates for the elevation of black identity. Consider the following lyrics of his song "African":

> So don't care where you come from
> As long as you're a black man, you're an African

No mind your complexion
There is no rejection, you're an African
'Cause if your plexion high, high, high
If your complexion low, low
And if your plexion in between, you're an African

Speaking of this song Hume and Heron (2012, 43) argue, "Expressing oneself as an African within the confines of Afro-Caribbean existence entails a commitment to consciousness and liberation, and to resistance against any form of domination." Tosh is combating the layers of colourism within society. He renders African heritage stronger than any other racial background. He exalts it over regional affiliation. This message is antithetical to the national agenda which highlights racial mixing and harmony. "There is no rejection" speaks directly to the attempt to dissociate Jamaican identity from African identity. The debasement of blackness is part of a neocolonial legacy that sickens this artist. The real problems with negative sentiment towards blackness and poorness lay in unjust state practices. It is important to consider that Tosh's stance against injustice often left him associated with other forms of social "badness". Speaking of the Wailers, for example, Masouri (2013, 42) explains "they defended the rude boys because they shared in their frustrations, and sided with them against police brutality". Tosh distances himself from rude boy culture at other times, but continues to be associated with civil disobedience.

I interrogate Peter Tosh's life, work and networks as they ultimately relate to his cultural legacy. Tosh is one example of several artists within reggae and in other genres who have offered their voices and stories to spiritually and musically combat social oppression. Since he educated himself on issues of black politics and social justice, Tosh sings, plays, operates and speaks for social change and radical deconstruction of colour privilege and oppression. By no means do I proclaim that all the answers to neocolonialist oppression are found in his works. In fact, his observations must be remembered as responses to a specific socio-historical realm of Jamaica that has transformed in many ways since his death. My aim is to locate new ways of seeing Peter Tosh, his messages, and networks and interrogate the ways he negotiates race, class and oppression in his particular context.

Tosh as Black Rasta Confronting White Bias and Threatening Racial Ideology

Peter Tosh is often described with such words as militant, defiant, having a harder edge and revolutionary, which must be understood as contrary to the middle-class Jamaican sensibilities of his era. I speak directly to his negotiations of colour and class in Jamaican society and frame Jamaica within postcolonial Caribbean colour politics. Speaking about the structures of colonialism and neocolonialism and their implications on West Indian societies, Lowenthal (1972, 117) states, "Cultural emulation reinforces the economics of race; to be white is not only to be well-to-do but to be admired; to be black is not simply to be generally poor but to be despised, and to despise oneself." Lowenthal (116) argues that, for centuries, the West Indian exemplar has been the white European. Tosh was also influenced by widespread transnational exchanges about black identities.

Tosh as Rastafari-influenced Reggae Revolutionary

Tosh embraced Rastafari which disputed the validity of white and brown rule and constantly strove for an acknowledgment of African heritage. As I have mentioned, his stance in favour of black consciousness was unfavourable for his perception in some circles that preferred selective embrace of African heritage. Tosh's early work with the Wailers included various genres including ska, rocksteady, R&B and soul covers. He was familiar with many genres of music and allowed them to contribute to his own sound, but reggae is largely the genre of his solo work.

While government officials did not always support all the values of Jamaican popular music, these forms were instrumental during Jamaican political campaigns. The Wailers travelled with the campaign "Caravan of Stars", which also became known as the "PNP Musical Bandwagon" (Masouri 2013, 73). Tosh was Rastafari-influenced and embraced the thoughts, meanings and values of a changing entity. Before, Rastafari did not become involved with politics, instead keeping a low profile. In the 1960s, with reggae's growing prevalence, young people started to grow dreadlocks even if they were not Rasta (96). This shift into popular culture created new distinctions between genuine Rastafari and those who would "try on" the appearance of Rastafari without understanding its principles. Tosh would be a vocal opponent to such use of Rastafari. He felt spiritually driven by Rastafari and often described his knowledge of himself and his purpose as connected to his devotion to Jah Rastafari.

Reimaging Himself in Jah's Image

Brathwaite (2004, 514) explains that, in the Caribbean, recognizing the artist or participant's relationship with the ancestral past (African or Amerindian) is "a movement of possession into present and future. Through this movement of possession we become ourselves, truly our own creators, discovering word for object, image for the Word." Tosh reached towards an ancestral past in Africa. This relationship empowered him to create himself in an image of dignified blacks as he spoke back to derogatory and racicst images of Jamaican blackness. The kinds of widespread images of black Jamaicans during the 1950s and 1960s represent them inaccurately. For instance, Mills discusses Ian Fleming's *Dr No*, published in 1958, in which James Bond is sent to Jamaica. Fleming characterizes black Jamaicans and contrasts them to the British, the Syrians, Indians, and Chinese saying that the "Jamaican is a kindly lazy man with the virtues and vices of a child. He lives on a very rich island but he doesn't get rich from it. He doesn't know how to and he's too lazy" (Mills 2010, 106). Tosh rejected both subtle and blatant negative representations of blackness. He rejected the Christian church and shared his distaste of the notion that the Lord washed people "whiter than snow". He would ask "How can I be washed whiter than snow when I'm a black man?" (Masouri 2013, 115).

Hume and Heron (2012, 36) argue that, "as a Rastafarian,[10] Tosh was among a group of women and men who refused to accept the image of God as white and discarded the psychological impact of such an image". Tosh was in a lifelong project to reimage and reimagine himself in the image of a divine creator. The process elevated his mind to reach into his storehouse of creativity. Creativity for Tosh was the outlet that united with resources to propel his self-determination into a notable level of success. Bunny Wailer captures Tosh's character as influenced by determination to define himself with dignity denied the black person.

> Hear me now, Peter was a very arrogant person . . . Don't violate Peter's rights, don't try to intimidate Peter, don't treat him like you want to make him squint or succumb to your type of intimidation. Peter is not that type of guy. Peter was a soldier and wasn't the kind of guy to be pitied. Don't feel sorry for him because even if he were brought down, he'd still say something to make you laugh and twist some words around, comically. And if he's wounded, then he'll still try and walk. (Masouri 2013, 67)

Bunny Wailer reveals the ways that Tosh used words to counteract the negative energy of various situations. His message is shaped by a need to be resilient.

As a reggae revolutionary, I place Tosh within two contexts; one within Rastafari and the other within a wider black radical tradition. The first context is relayed in *Stepping Razor: Red X* in a scene with Bongo Israel, a Nyabinghi elder, who explains one of the notions of sonic power espoused by Rastafari saying, "word, sound and power. Word, sound and power is the symbol of man, seen. That's what we use amongst Babylon. We doesn't use a stick, nor a stone nor a gun" (Campbel 1993). Tosh showed his awareness of these kinds of sonic power regularly and even named his band Word, Sound and Power. His work is a part of a network of reggae sounds that seek to chant down Babylon. Tosh held a particular set of beliefs about the range of sonic power. A popular characterization of Tosh and several other revolutionary artists is one that asserts that they use their words as weapons. Tosh's lyrical weapons had a specific spiritual inflection. Esther Anderson, who co-wrote the first version of "Get Up, Stand Up" with Bob Marley, explains that Peter Tosh's additions were clear because of his unique style of speaking. Specifically, she notes, "that last verse about 'die and go to heaven in Jesus' name', that is definitely Peter's voice" (Masouri 2013, 114). According to Omar Davies (2000, 8), Peter Tosh's "Get Up! Stand Up!" versions on the *Equal Rights* and *Captured Live* albums "convey to the listener his anger, his intolerance of social injustice, in a much more forceful manner than the versions of his colleagues".

I relate his forceful manner of speech and song to the black radical imaginary. Anthony Bogues (2003, 10) writes about "two major streams of black radical intellectual production – the heretic and the prophetic". The heretic refers to highly educated individuals and prophetic to "religious" men and women. I focus on one feature of those in prophetic strain of black radical imaginary: "The third feature to note of this redemptive stream is its creative usage of language to describe social conditions and affirm their humanity. In these instances the word – *la parole* – become a weapon, a chant, and an invocation beating against the walls of oppression as well as an illocutionary force" (20).

I focus on the last portion of this phrase about "illocutionary force". One can understand this term by thinking first about how any speech act is "constative" and "performative"; it declares and it performs. It says something and dramatizes something. The illocutionary force that Bogues mentions has to do with the way a speech act performs something, what Lawrence Kramer describes as "the pressure or power that a speech act exerts on a situation" (1990, 7). I frame my analysis of his spoken word and lyrics in terms of what he is declaring but more importantly, how his statements are performing pressure. Let us now seek to locate the dimensions of language and force that Tosh employed by using Jamaican curse words in speech and song.

Peter Tosh's Subversive and Taboo Speech Acts and Social Change

Peter Tosh is described as a wordsmith. Taitu Heron and Yanique Hume (2012, 27) contextualize his wordworks, saying, "Wordworks is a performative, embodied act of consciously being able to use the creative imagination to transform language and the English use of words, altering meaning and thus making it political." Two of Tosh's famous taboo wordworks are *shitstem* and *shituation* which operationalize counterhegemonic stances. They speak against the postcolonial society which leaves major portions of Jamaica's population disenfranchised.

Omar Davies, former member of parliament and government minister, explains that Tosh's liberal use of such words is part of the reason why he is not recognized with the same honour as Bob Marley (Tulloch 2013, 59). These words, along with his strong advocacy for legitimizing ganja and his confrontations with the police, marked him as an opponent to "decency". As Dennis Thompson describes it, there exists a prevailing image of Tosh "as a miserable and cantankerous person" though "he was nothing like that in real life" (Tulloch 2013, 116–17). In Omar Davies's contribution to Ceil

Tulloch's volume *Remembering Peter Tosh*, he questions the appropriateness of the venue of the One Love Peace Concert for Tosh's infamous expletive-filled frontal attack on political leaders. Others like Desmond Shakespeare explained that when Tosh began to lace this particular "livatribe" (versus diatribe) with profanity it turned off many people in the audience. Shakespeare believed the audience's focus shifted to his delivery and away from his message (Tulloch 2013, 36). Davies offers that Tosh may have been resisting social norms that made silly words indecent (60). I argue that his point may prove to be a parallel factor but I would revise use of the word *silly* because it minimizes the power Tosh believes such words have. Indeed, his delivery is integral to his message.

Carolyn Cooper (2012) offers this analysis of Tosh's coined phrases which infuse curse words into state structures: "The words 'system' and 'situation' were cleverly transformed by the addition of a well-placed 'h' and 't'. Tosh evoked the stench of the oppressive dunghills of social injustice and moral corruption that continue to rise up everywhere in Jamaica." Here she exposes the metaphoric power and truth in his use of profanity. Cooper (2013) also invokes Tosh in an article which considers the possible divine origins of the curse word *bumbaclaat*. Her central argument is that many Jamaican curse words refer to "perfectly good female body parts and functions" yet their African origins makes it difficult to appreciate "the explosive power" of these words both positive and negative. She would not dismiss these bad words as "devaluation of women" but as "sign of the potency of female sexuality". Cooper (2013) shares some of James Drummond-Hay's letter to the editor in which speculated that the word *bumbaclaat* may have come from the Boshongo people of central Africa. The god in one of their creation narratives is named Bumba and, by Drummond-Hay's speculation, like a person in Christian society would exclaim "O God", Boshongo people may say "O Bumba"; the task left would be to determine what ties exists between Jamaica and central Africa. Cooper (2013) goes on to explain that this spiritual perspective converges with her sexualized analysis.

Cooper's 1983 interview with Tosh reveals that he was confounded by the ways people will use other curse words but get vexed particularly at *bumbaclaat*. He described it as having "too much spirituality". He referred to the numerous verses he wrote to clarify in his song "O Bumbo Klaat" because "middle-class nice, decent, clean people out there don't like that" (Cooper 2012). He also expressed frustration that the persons trying to silence him do devious acts in society. These are the kinds of contradictions that give Tosh what Rex Nettleford described as a "noble rage".

Jamaica's Towns and Communities Act includes a law against use of indecent language under section 9c. The section outlaws writing, drawing, painting, representing, singing, or using obscene and indecent representations or language. Periodically, cases bring the colonial remnant under scrutiny, such as the 2012 murder of Kay-Ann Lamont (*Jamaica Observer*, 3 September 2012) and Sizzla's $1,000 fine in 2014 (*Gleaner*, 16 March 2014). Tosh's habitual defiance of this neocolonial prohibition is crucial to his position as a black radical prophet. In a conversation with Peter Simon, Tosh explains: "Well, I was born and raised and grown up in colonialism and exploitation, and I heard that bumboclaat, Rassclaat, bloodclaat and every kind of claat you could think of is bad word and indecent language. They're banned here in Jamaica but why is it indecent?" (Masouri 2013, 303–4). Tosh questions why these words are problematic but also reveals the answer by naming colonialism and exploitation. Cooper and Drummond-Hay's exchange names the other side of the answer because it portrays *bumbaclaat*'s positive and negative powers and identifies its cultural emergence from African heritage. By analysing Tosh's language, I reveal more closely how Jamaica's colonial order demeaned blackness by devaluing African-influenced language, and that, in turn, the neocolonial Jamaican nationalist government extended this pattern.

Language and Power Contextualization of the Importance of Patois for Tosh

In Jamaica, the language of the black masses, patwah (or patois), and the official language, English, have a contested relationship (Carr 1994, 135). Patois is referred to as a dialect. Yet this description is underlined with notions of power. In fact, all languages are dialects; the official language can be understood as the dialect with an army. Money and status makes one dialect standard. Patois is often framed as "bad English", because the language's lexical items are drawn largely from English while it operates on different, namely African-influenced, grammatical structures. The Jamaican Language Unit at the Mona Campus of the University of the West Indies has been working to standardize Jamaican patois and improve its status. The unit calls for bilingual education as well as use of patois in government processes. The vertical variation between patois and Jamaican standard English mark differences in socio-economic background, status, educational background, race, ethnicity and so on. The words that are central to my argument further add to the notion of vertical variation in language because when one uses taboo words you are considered not to have "broughtupcy", a colloquial term for social decency. Both patois and Jamaican curse words reside in a linguistic group that is stigmatized in various ways despite being linked to history, communal memory and everyday interactions. Hume and Heron (2012, 29) argue that "embracing African and African diasporic identifiers, to inform the discipline, would necessitate entertaining areas where English is simply not chosen as the sole communicative medium and even more so, where the English language alone is recognised as being inadequate to convey the realities of Caribbean existence".

Heron and Hume (29) include Tosh's important explanation of the limitations of English: "I don't like to talk English because there is something else trying to come out . . . but dat was de education, zeen?" They explain that because the political underpinnings of colonial and neocolonial society have framed "African as inferior", the creole language operates at the margins of society (29). He uses the language of frustrated people living in the margins to launch lyrical critiques.

According to Martinican psychoanalyst Frantz Fanon (1968, 1–2): "To speak means to be in a position to use a certain syntax, to grasp the morphology of this or that language, but it means above all to assume a culture, to support the weight of a civilization." By contesting the use of English, Tosh is contesting the culture of European colonizers. In his analysis of race in Antillean culture, Fanon notes that "a black man behaves differently with a white man than he does with another black man" (1). This is true for Tosh's use of language in some instances. When speaking with international audiences, Tosh uses standard English so that he may be understood, but when speaking passionately, creole words and structures prevail. For example, in an interview discussing the prevalence of commercial music and obstacles to his own music's success, Tosh says, "That not gwine change me, because I am going to kill the fuckery out there, and people is going to be in demand for the truth" (Abbott 2012c). Tosh goes on to criticize the kinds of songs with popularity saying "I sick and tired of hearing that bumbo bloodclaat!" and he receives applause from his largely non-Jamaican audience (Abbott 2012c).

Di Claat Dem: Bumbaclaat and Rasclaat

When Desmond Shakespeare asked Peter Tosh why he wrote this song "Oh Bumbo Klaat", Tosh responded that many people were curious about the meaning of Jamaican expletives and he was enlightening them (Tulloch 2013, 36). I draw attention to one verse which summarizes the deeper dimensions of Tosh's thoughts about curse words, particularly *bumbaclaat*.

> One night, an evil spirit held me down
> I could not make one single sound
> Jah told me, "Son, use the word"
> And now I'm as free as a bird
> Oh bumbo klaat, oh ras klaat

In this verse, Tosh asserts that curse words can free a person from evil forces. In *Stepping Razor: Red X*, Peter Tosh tells a story behind this claim. He begins by describing a moment in which he feels paralysed in his bed, held down by an evil spirit. He began to make inner communication within himself. This inner communication gave him confidence in the notion of a creator living within man. Then, he asked the Creator what to do and the voice responded

> You just say "Move yuh bomboclaat." Ignoring his confusion at the instruction, the creator began a countdown. Tosh describes: "In the countdown is like ah heard 3 . . . 2 . . . and when 1 go seh I say 'Move you' (and when I say) 'bumbaclaat' it just fly out like bam! 'BUMBACLAAT.' Immediately every spell was released . . . this is why people say that this is indecent language so they can use these words to release their vampires on you." (Campbel 1993)

With this explanation in mind, one can now frame his use of curse words as aimed to release his vampires on the status quo. One can connect the use of *bumbaclaat* back to his story and see how using the word dispelled evil forces. The singing of this word repeatedly is part of a deeper personal expression. Gregory Sandow, speaking of Sinatra (particularly towards his mean personality that is shown in Kitty Kelley's unauthorized biography), problematizes people's attempt to separate the artist from the man: "Because he *is* an artist, he can't help telling a kind of truth; he can't help reaching towards the root of everything he's felt" (Frith 1996, 186). Tosh is tapping into this power to drive out evil because he has felt it work.

The word is also tied with his internalization of spiritual faith; faith not in the sense that there was a god or creator "out there" but one that lived in him. His elucidation of *bumbaclaat*'s power coincided with an important act of acknowledging Jah within him, which becomes a lifelong project. The moment and the word become interconnected with his sense that Jah "sent [him] here to help alleviate the shitstem. . . . The terrible filth and corruption." They become tied with an inner creative force which showed him how to help himself (Campbel 1993).

There are other moments in which it is clear that his use of *bumbaclaat* is tied to a discursive relationship that involves all his experiences (physical, spiritual and mental). In an interview responding to the manner in which his record company, managers and distributors worked to ignore the demand of fans for his music and live performances, Peter Tosh says, "But is not a Michael Jackson bumboclaat element and not a likkle um (weh di next one name) Prince element and dem kin'a likkle bit bat bumboclaat element, weh yu say, it too black fi dem" (Semayat 2009).

Here, the word *black* refers to the appearance of the pop stars and the consciousness of the music. Tosh belittles popular black music for not being black enough. He also distinguishes himself as a more militant advocate for blackness. He is always invested in turning black inferiority on its head. Tosh frames his agenda in black music as more noble than Michael Jackson's and Prince's commercially successful styles, although one cannot deny that both artists performed songs crying for human dignity, such as Jackson's "Man in the Mirror" and Prince's "When Will We Be Paid".

The song "Oh Bumbo Klaat" uses the pairing of *bumbaclaat* and *rassclaat*. Peter Tosh explains his experience of realizing himself as illegitimate child in *Reggae Routes*: "Me is what them call illegitimate, that mean say me is a criminal, [bumba] rassclaat! That's why me [a] go do a song called

'Illegitimate Children'" (Masouri 2013, 8). The words are used to throw sonic power against the prejudices and active criminalization of children born out of wedlock. Additionally, he uses rassclat to assault the notion of black skin inferiority: "I have no mother here, I have a *bearer*... Jah is my mother and Jah is my father. My earthly parents don't know my potential or my divine qualities. They weren't taught to diagnose or be aware of such things. They were looking at skin complexion and because me born so rassclaat black, she know me was a curse according to the shit-stem them times there" (Masouri 2013, 9–10).

When he uses the word *rassclaat*, Tosh juxtaposes the deprecating view of society with his sureness in his own divinity. Tosh presents an ideology that was within the stiches of everyday exchanges. He pre-emptively overturns the idea that he can be a curse. He conveys a certain force in blackness. "Rassclaat black" is the hegemonic reading of dark skin that he exposes with the vulgar term. Together, the words are aimed at destroying the "downpressive" structures within Jamaican society.

>It's been so long
>We need a change
>So the shitstem we got to rearrange
>And if there's obstacles in the road, we got to throw them overboard
>Oh bumbo klaat, oh ras klaat
>Oh bumbo klaat, oh ras klaat

At the foundation of his use of profanity is the desire to rid Jamaica of profane practices. Dismissing his critiques for lack of decorum is dangerous. The obstacles in the way will find new ways to reproduce themselves if this decency distraction remains a prevailing discourse. His words imply a context of forward movement and national progress. They provide a vision of the entire nation being caught up in "noble rage" singing "Oh bumbo klaat, oh ras klaat" as an expression of that, now productive, anger.

An End to Shitty Structures?[11]

In a 1986 interview in New York, Peter Tosh shared his frustrations with management or, as he dubbed them, "damagement". Tosh spoke about the music business structure that exploits the artist. After one interviewer asked why his distributors would not release one of his performance videos, despite the demand for it in the United States, Tosh erupted in a rhythmic performance of Jamaican curse words and noble rage. He declared: "These are the tings dat I bumbaclaat talk about. And when I get so fucking upset I don bodda bloodclaat talk English bumbaclaat grammar cau'e dem ting deh get mi very bumbaclaat upset! Seen" (Abbott 2012b). Tosh reveals that he cannot communicate in English when infuriated by these biased structures. He rails against "get down shake your booty" songs and singing "I love you" and insists that he is resolved to not be changed from the artist he is. Tosh emphasizes that people are tired of hearing the same thing; they want truth (Abbott 2012b).

Peter Tosh's use of profanity cannot be separated from his concern for social change. Carolyn Cooper (2012) argues that "Tosh evoked the stench of the oppressive dung hills of social injustice and moral corruption that continue to rise up everywhere in Jamaica". Tosh's work re-presents the ways that neocolonial structures reimpose the certain geographies of socio-economic prosperity and decay. "Oppressive dung hills" must first be produced from ingesting. The privileged eat their fill, and money and power keep their streets and pathways pristine. The disenfranchised eke out their portions, but waste accumulates in their districts. Tosh's words draw attention to the ways "many youths in general become victims of the shitstem". He remarks: "O the pain. Many I see die because of impatience. I see many get frustrated, kinky, crack, nuts, crazy walking out of themselves. Lost into fantasy, seeking to find the reality, and I see myself in the same situation" (Campbel 1993). His subversion is concerned with the real consequences of inequality. To dismiss his observation for decorum sake neglects the lack of decorum in social injustice.

In his song "Ha Fe Get a Beating" (1968), he elaborates on the structures of society that need to be addressed:

> Due to unfavourable financial conditions,
> I am unable to cope with this financial shituation,
> It's causing an inflation upon creation.

He writes this song six years after independence when financial problems persist and official institutions attempt to address them. For instance, the 1972–1980 Michael Manley government had sought to address unemployment by setting up "work schemes for the unskilled" (Masouri 2013, 95). As in several of his songs, Tosh's thesis is that poor people are set up to cope, to tread out a living with cobweb stability.

In the final analysis, it is necessary to understand that while Tosh also used curse words to belittle, shame and embarrass people, the efficacy of word choice depends on the context. Cursing societal structures often overlapped with cursing his unstable business and friendship relationships. Yet, I argue that in many cases his curse against social injustice should be understood above interpersonal emotion. Tosh explains his reasons for leaving the Wailers: "It's not a matter of being in conflict with Bob. It's just being in conflict with the shituation I live in my whole life approximately, and it defamates my character and belittles my authority, underestimates my ability and me couldn't stomach that for another twelve years" (Campbel 1993). He elevates his frustration from individual to societal. As a lifelong target of anti-black inferiority language, Tosh implicates the structures that surround him.

Several individuals were disturbed by Tosh's *livatribe* at the One Love Peace Concert because of its use of curse words and the disrespect shown to high-ranking officials in attendance. I would point out that his portrayal of politicians is slightly more nuanced. Tosh conceptualizes government officials as those who mechanize evil against the poor but also points beyond them to a spiritual reproduction of exploitive practices, saying "irrespective of what's going on now and what government is in power, government have to know that you have a whole lot of evil forces to fight who don't like to see nothing progressive" (Shamrock08 2010). Tosh's use of curse words works in tandem with a larger hope to transform Jamaican society, despite the strong legacies of exploitation and oppression.

Peter Tosh says this of himself: "If I wasn't a singer I'd be a bloodclaat revolutionary. I'd be killing bumbaclaat wicked everyday" (Campbel 1993). His statement reveals that curse words are versatile. They assign power to either positive concepts like revolution or negative forces like wicked (in line with Carolyn Cooper's argument). Tosh also characterizes his destruction of the *shitstem* in violent ways, for example, using the verb "kill". This analysis considered the ways that curse words allow Tosh to verbally assault social injustice and call for social change.

But, I ask further, does he truly kill all the injustice? To conclude, I think about the ways that Tosh's cultural legacy also reveals other forms of social inequality. While Tosh creates a symbolic order in his critiques of racism and classism, this battle for complete human validation is not fully extended to women and non-heterosexual people. That is, the obvious decolonizing potential of Tosh's work does not eclipse its misogyny and homophobia. I call for further inquiry seeking to analyse Peter Tosh's life, work and networks as they ultimately relate to his vision of social justice and its limitations in terms of gender and sexuality. Such a line of questioning proves necessary particularly in the recent debates around reggae's successor, dancehall. Dancehall has been contrasted to reggae of the 1970s and 1980s, when abstracted as a cornerstone of love for all people.[12]

Tosh is one example of several artists within reggae and in other genres who have offered their voices and stories to spiritually and musically combat social oppression. Since he educated himself in issues of black politics and social justice, Tosh sings, plays, operates and speaks for social change and radical deconstruction of colour privilege and oppression. Yet, all the answers to neocolonialist oppression are not found in his works. In fact, his observations must be remembered as responses to a specific sociohistorical realm of Jamaica that has transformed in many ways since his death. He is implicated by the prejudices of his era, prejudices that have resonance in contemporary critiques of dancehall. His black radical output frames freedom while recreating gender and sexuality oppression.

When a reporter asks Peter Tosh to elaborate on his statement that he is tired of love songs, Tosh first distinguishes songs that say "I love you" from love songs (which are in his repertoire, however rarely). He then goes on to say he is

> sick and tired of hearing a guy telling a girl that him love her. You tell her that in bumbaclaat bed. Yu haffi sing to ar? And this is why the society is so fucking bizarre man and everything going bumbaclaat upside down because a man going cry bloodclaat tears a sing to some girl ah tell ar she him love ar. . . . I am not a homo-bloodclaat-sexual; I tell a woman that in bed. (Abbott 2012c)

Tosh's words signal a number of problematic gender and sexuality stereotypes. First, he forecloses expressing love towards women to the space of heterosexual intercourse. He renders heterosexuality the only normal ontology by saying "the society is so fucking bizarre" and "upside down". Tosh expresses an uncompromising expectation of gender roles as natural rather than gender roles as maintained by being continually performed. He misses what Judith Butler (1993, 340) describes: heterosexism is promoted by heteronormative social regimes.

Vivien Goldman describes Peter Tosh's sexist attitudes, which she encountered in many ways, including a direct comment that "if she was menstruating, then she would have to keep her distance" (Masouri 2013, 238). In an interview, Bruno Blum asks Tosh whether women should have equal rights as men. Tosh answers by calling on stereotypical codes of women being weaker than men and women being created for the comfort of man. He also provides a list of Old Testament–derived prohibitions and delimitations for women's bodies – that is, not wearing men's clothing and isolation during menstruation. He says, "A man must not sleep with a woman when she stays that way [on her period]. Babylon or western philosophy tells you that is all right but the Rastaman says no, and the Rastaman's culture is the traditional black culture, seen?" (Masouri 2013, 238–39). Normative black culture in this constellation does little to promote what I consider a sustainable vision of decolonial social justice.

As a final meditation, I present Tosh's lyrics from "The Poor Man Feel It":

> Only the poor man a feel it, yeah ah!
> Only him feel it, oh ah!
> Only the poor man a feel it, every time!
> Only the poor man a feel it, yeah ah . . .

This is precisely the limit. Overall, Tosh spearheads necessary class critique and calls for social justice for "poor people". Yet, it can be argued that his vision for full empowerment remains for the poor cis-male heterosexual first.

Notes

1. "Shitstem" is a word Tosh is known to have coined. It refers to neocolonial systems that frustrate the potential of poor black people to operate without bias and limits against them.
2. A turn of the phrase for "diatribes" used to describe Peter Tosh's statements during performances. These are integral to the performance and weave together his song choices. The study focuses on moments when he speaks directly to social injustice, political power, and social awareness.
3. Thomas (2004, 71) further describes the Henry Rebellion, an armed resistance against colonial, impending nationalist government and security forces to establish and black government and ultimately repatriate to Africa.
4. Ledgister parahrasing Obika Gray, *Radicalism and Social Change in Jamaica*.
5. Walter Rodney, a Black Power advocate, taught at the University of the West Indies and routinely outlined the need for black men and women in Jamaica to feel in control of their destinies. Rodney, a Guyanese-born scholar, cited the near-omnipresent nature of black oppression: "in our own homelands we have no power, abroad we are discriminated against, and everywhere the black masses suffer in poverty" (Weeks 2008, 53). Some argue that, fearing Rodney's words had hidden agendas with Castro politics, the Jamaican government banned him from lecturing at the University of the West Indies and from returning to Jamaica in 1968. Others note the government's concern that his presence would affect the tourist market. The ban incited riots among students and urban youth.
6. The Green Bay Massacre refers to 5 January 1978 when the Jamaica Defence Force soldiers killed five men from the Central Kingston community of Southside. One of the five men who escaped the incident, Delroy Anthony Griffiths, reports that they were lured into a trap by men who promised them jobs paying three hundred dollars a week (H.G. Helps, "Death Postponed", *Jamaica Observer*, 15 April 2012).
7. Subsection adapted from Bernard (2015b).
8. See Abbott (2012a).
9. According to Ken Gelder, "subcultures are groups of people that in some way represented as non-normative and/or marginal through their particular interests and practices, through what they are and where they do it" (2005, 1).
10. Rastafarian and Rastafarianism are terms that many Rastafari do not embrace. However, the terms are often used in academia.
11. This section extends prior work of Bernard (2015a, 2015c).
12. See Kohlings and Lilly (2013), Noble (2008), and Smith and Kosobucki (2011).

References

Abbott, Ronnie. 2012a. "Peter Tosh – Interview Part 3". YouTube. 5 April. https://www.youtube.com/watch?v=VrGorril-Ss.

———. 2012b. "Peter Tosh - Interview Part 4". YouTube. 5 April. https://www.youtube.com/watch?v=PeSvdExRp5Y.

———. 2012c. "Peter Tosh - Interview Part 5". YouTube. 5 April. https://www.youtube.com/watch?v=viLjwoJzSgA.

archives, m. 2014. *Peter Tosh Behind the Music*. YouTube. 19 June. https://www.youtube.com/watch?v=FkZ8VHh8tvA.

Aylmer, Kevin. 1987. "Epilogue: The Passing of Peter Tosh: Jamaica's Bush Doctor Flies Away Home". *Reggae and African Beat*, November, 20–22, 30.

Balsini, Gilberto M. 2009. "Caribbean Cinematic Créolité". *Black Camera* 1 (1): 70–90.

Balutansky, Kathleen M., and Marie-Agnés Sourieau. 1998. *Caribbean Creolization: Reflections on the Cultural Dynamics of Language, Literature and Identity*. Kingston: University of the West Indies Press.

Bernard, Racquel. 2015a. "Dancehall and Homophobia: Listening and Activism across International Differences". Report for Jamaica Forum for Lesbians, All-Sexuals and Gays.

———. 2015b. "Naming Natty and Negotiating Natural: Black Hair Styles in Jamaican Discourse". Typescript.

———. 2015c. "Sounds of Reggae Revolution: Revisiting Peter Tosh's Cultural Legacy". Master's research project. July.

Bogues, Anthony. 2003. *Black Heretics and Black Power*. New York: Routledge.

———. 2009. "Black Power, Decolonization, and Caribbean Politics: Walter Rodney and the Politics of the Groundings with My Brothers". *Boundary* 2:127–47.

Brathwaite, Kamau. 2004. "Timehri". In *The Birth of Caribbean Civilisation: A Century of Ideas about Culture and Identity, Nation and Society*, edited by N. Bolland, 504–15. Kingston: Ian Randle.

Brown-Glaude, Winnefred. 2007. "The Fact of Blackness? The Bleached Body in Contemporary Jamaica". *Small Axe* 11 (3): 34–51.

Butler, Judith. 1993. "Subjects of Sex/Gender/Desire". In *The Cultural Studies Reader*, edited by S. During, 340–53. New York: Routledge.

Campbel, Nicholas, dir. 1993. *Stepping Razor: Red X*. YouTube. https://www.youtube.com/watch?v=JNJ0b98bI10&list=PLB4C56255315F0FED (part 1 of 10).

Carr, Robert. 1994. "Struggles from the Periphery: Sistren and the Politics of Subaltern Autobiography". *Dispositio* 19 (46): 127–45.

Cooper, Carolyn. 2012. "Peter Tosh Did Not Joke with Words". *Gleaner*, 14 October.

———. 2013. "Divine Jamaican Bad Words". *Gleaner*, 8 September.

Davies, Omar. 2000. *Reggae and Our National Identity: The Forgotten Contribution of Peter Tosh*. Kingston, JA: Pear Tree Press.

Despestre, René. 2004. "Problems of Identity for the Black Man in Caribbean Literatures". In *The Birth of Caribbean Civilisation: A Century of Ideas about Culture and identity, Nation and Society*, edited by N. Bolland, 236–49. Kingston: Ian Randle.

Fanon, Frantz. 1968. *Black Skin, White Masks*. New York: Grove Press.

Frith, Simon. 1996. *Performing Rites: On the Value of Popular Music*. Cambridge, MA: Harvard University Press.

Gelder, Ken. 2005. "Introduction: The Field of Subcultural Studies". In *The Subcultures Reader* edited by Ken Gelder and Sarah Thornton, 1–18. London: Routlegde.

GNDGeneral. 2011. "Peter Tosh @ Sky Channel [1987]". YouTube. 9 September. https://www.youtube.com/watch?v=ywuZDbpwMzQ.

Hanchard, Michael. 2008. "Black Memory Versus State Memory: Notes toward a Method". *Small Axe* 12 (2): 45–62.

Heron, Taitu, and Yanique Hume. 2012. "Stepping Out: Peter Tosh and Dynamics of Afro-Caribbean Existence". *Caribbean Quarterly* 58 (4): 25–49.

Hintzen, Perry. 2002. "Race and Creole Ethnicity in the Caribbean". In *Questioning Creole: Creolisation Discourse in Caribbean Culture*, edited by V. Shepherd and G.L. Richards, 92–110. Kingston: Ian Randle.

Helps, HG. "VIDEO: Death Postponed - Green Bay Survivor Reflects: Green Bay — The Worst Thing That Ever Happened to Me." April 15, 2012. Jamaica Observer.

Hope, Donna P. 2011. "From Browning to Cake Soap: Popular Debates on Skin Bleaching in the Jamaican Dancehall". *Journal of Pan-African Studies* 4 (4): 165–94.

King, Steven A. 2002. *Reggae, Rastafari, and the Rhetoric of Social Control*. Jackson: University Press of Mississippi.

Kohlings, Ellen, and Pete Lilly. 2013. "From One Love to One Hate?" In *International Reggae: Current and Future Trends in Jamaican Popular Music*, by Donna P. Hope, 2–29. Kingston: Pelican Publishers.

Kramer, Lawrence. 1990. *Music as Cultural Practice, 1800–1900*. Berkeley: University of California Press.

Ledgister, F.S.J. 2008. " 'Intellectual Murder':Walter Rodney's Groundings in the Jamaican Context". *Commonwealth and Comparative Politics* 46 (1): 79–100.

Lowenthal, David. 1972. "Black Power in the Caribbean Context". *Economic Geography* 48 (1): 116–34.

Masouri, John. 2013. *The Life of Peter Tosh Steppin' Razor*. London: Omnibus.

Mathes, Carter. 2010. "Circuits of Political Prophecy: Martin Luther King Jr., Peter Tosh, and the Black Radical Imaginary". *Small Axe* 14 (2): 17–41.

Mills, Charles W. 2010. *Radical Theory Caribbean Reality: Race, Class and Social Domination*. Kingston: University of the West Indies Press.

Nettleford, Rex. 2004. "National Identity and Attitudes to Race in Jamaica". In *The Birth of Caribbean Civilisation: A Century of Ideas about Culture and Identity, Nation and Society*, edited by N. Bolland, 461–73. Kingston: Ian Randle.

Noble, Denise. 2008. "Postcolonial Criticism, Transnational Identification and Hegemonies of Dancehall's Academic and Performatives". *Feminist Review* no. 90: 106–27.

oravcik. 2011. "Peter Tosh Montreal Interview Part 1, 1983". YouTube. 31 July. https://www.youtube.com/watch?v=qYM5SlWrr7w.

Semayat. 2009. "Peter Tosh Interview - New York 1986". YouTube. 10 January. https://www.youtube.com/watch?v=eQPGKaqfBY8

Shamrock08. 2010. "Peter Tosh - Speech at the One Love Peace Concert 1978". YouTube. 9 March. https://www.youtube.com/watch?v=dwZnX5JB8q4.

Smithsonian Folkways. 2003. "Artist Spotlight: Bernice Johnson Reagon Civil Rights Song Leader". 22 October. YouTube. https://www.youtube.com/watch?v=dK-KejG4j3P0.

Thomas, Deborah A. 2004. *Modern Blackness: Nationalism, Globalization and the Politics of Culture in Jamaica*. Durham, NC: Duke University Press.

Tulloch, Ceil, ed. 2013. *Remembering Peter Tosh*. Kingston: Ian Randle.

Weeks, D. 2008. "Movement of the People: The Relationship between Black Consciousness, Race, and Class in the Caribbean". Master's thesis, University of South Forida.

CHAPTER 5

A KARTEL OF SIN?
Messianic Desires and Vybz

ANNA KASAFI PERKINS

> "That Kartel is a messy man, fi true."
> —Nichole C in response to Messiah in "Season of Fear"

Leading up to and in the wake of his trial and conviction for murder in 2014, the responses to the Vybz Kartel story were myriad and varied, including cartoons, newspaper columns, songs and social media content. (See, for example, Helber [2012], which presents a compelling analysis of *Jamaica Observer* editorial cartoons on Kartel.) Kartel even features prominently in a portrait in the National Gallery of Jamaica done by Vermont "Howie" Grant, entitled *Dance Hall Artistes (rgb)* (separating arch-rivals Beenie Man and Bounty Killer [2014]).[1] One rarely explored source of commentary on the Vybz Kartel phenomenon has been poetry. Nicholas Alexander, an up-and-coming Jamaican poet, whose work has been published in the Jamaican *Sunday Observer*, penned a poem entitled "Season of Fear" in which he reflects on and critiques the Kartel phenomenon using strongly Christian language and allusion. In so doing, Alexander examines the question of Kartel's Messiah-like status in the eyes of many, especially the urban poor.

This chapter undertakes a brief literary analysis of the Alexander poem, excavating themes and images to show how Alexander echoes meanings given to the Kartel phenomenon, which was on trial. The messianic desires of some of the Jamaican populace, who are often on the lookout for a messiah

A KARTEL OF SIN? MESSIANIC DESIRES AND VYBZ

(for example, a politician or "world boss"), are also interrogated and Kartel's self-understanding, as presented in his co-authored prison reflections *The Voice of the Jamaican Ghetto* (Palmer and Dawson 2012), is briefly examined. The chapter concludes by questioning the continued existence of and need for messianic figures among the Jamaican populace and the ambiguity of Kartel's own messianic self-identity.

Vybz Kartel

Jamaican dancehall artiste Vybz Kartel, born Adidja Azim Palmer on 7 January 1976, rose to global prominence in 2003 with the release of his debut album *Up 2 Di Time* and a headline-grabbing "clash" with veteran dancehall deejay Ninjaman at Sting.[2] This was on the heels of Kartel being declared deejay of the year in 2002 at the Stone Love thirtieth anniversary party. Being crowned deejay of the year at that event signalled that Kartel had arrived on the local dancehall scene.

Kartel fell in love with music early, having uncles who made less-than-successful forays into the dancehall arena and a mother who supported his interests and budding talent. He skipped school regularly to be in the studio and he was eventually expelled from Calabar High School for indiscipline. His first recording, the single "Love Fat Woman" on the One Heart label, was made at the age of seventeen under the stage name Adi Banton.[3] Three years later, in 1996, he formed a group with two friends under the name Vybz Cartel after watching a movie about the exploits of Columbian drug lord Pablo Escobar and his drug cartel. Kartel soon launched out on his own while keeping the group's name as his own moniker, but with a slight change in spelling. Shortly after launching his solo career, he became a protégé of popular dancehall artiste Bounty Killer. As a part of Bounty Killer's Alliance team, Kartel penned lyrics for other prominent artistes, including Elephant Man. He also did a number of local collaborations with Bounty Killer, including songs like "Gal Clown" and "Girls Like Mine", which were instant hits on the dancehall scene. Hit after hit followed and he was soon a household name in Jamaica with a growing fan base, especially among the youth.

Kartel broke away from Bounty Killer's Alliance team in 2006[4] and began a very public feud with his former mentor and Bounty's new protégé Mavado. Mavado was identified with the community of Cassava Piece, also known as "Gully", in St Andrew, from which he hailed. Several years later, then-prime minister Bruce Golding was forced to call both Mavado and Kartel to a meeting to negotiate a cessation to the escalating violence resulting from their ongoing feud, known as the Gaza versus Gully feud. Based on the intensity of this Gaza versus Gully feud, the reputed don Christopher "Dudus" Coke planned a peace concert featuring both artistes, but this was cancelled by the minister of culture (https://www.allmusic.com/artist/vybz-kartel-mn0000261309/biography).

As his career ballooned, Kartel developed a massive following, especially among young people, both locally and internationally. He later formed his own empire – the Gaza Empire – and produced other successful dancehall artistes from Portmore, including Jah Vinci, Gaza Slim, Popcaan and Sheba.[5] A talented lyricist and performer, Kartel was often described as controversial (Toppin 2011), "somewhat of a phenomenon" and "the Pied Piper [drawing students away from class]" (editorial, *Sunday Observer*, 16 March 2014). He was globally recognized and engaged in collaborations with artistes like Jay-Z and Rihanna, featuring on the latter's hit single "What's My Name". Other musical collaborators included Missy Elliot, Busta Rhymes,[6] Akon and Eminem. Gender specialist Danielle Toppin (2011) describes this dancehall star thus:

> Vybz Kartel has become a defining force in the Caribbean landscape of dancehall music. With often sexually explicit and violent lyrics, he has remained a controversial figurehead within the local music industry, a trend that has intensified with his defence of skin bleach [sic]; evidenced by his steadily lightening skin. So strong has the association been, that Kartel himself launched not only a hugely successful song about cake soap (reportedly used as a skin lightener), but a "cake soap" skin product.

Such was his popularity that Kartel's endorsement in song was enough to send sales of Clarks shoes soaring in Jamaica.[7] He was also a serial entrepreneur and ventured into commercial activities such as his own brand of cake soap and shoes, Vybz rum, and Daggerin condoms. Kartel was the first dancehall artiste to star in his own reality show titled *Teacha's Pet*, which aired briefly on local television and is archived online. In 2011, he was given the honour of delivering a lecture at the Mona campus of the University of the West Indies.⁸

During his career, accolades aplenty were heaped on him. For example, Max Glazer of New York's Federation Sound System comments that "Vybz Kartel is certainly one of the most important and influential artists in the history of dancehall.... When you talk about someone having total mastery over the art of deejaying and total control over the psyche and consciousness of dancehall worldwide" (Fernando 2014).

All this came crashing down in 2011 when Kartel was arrested and charged for the murder of Barrington "Bosie" Burton, a music promoter. He made bail on the Burton murder charge but was never able to take it up as he was remanded in custody for the murder of Clive "Lizard" Williams. He was convicted and sentenced for this crime in 2014. In the wake of his sentencing, his case continues to be dissected and stories of his alleged acts of violence have come thick and fast.⁹ Nonetheless, based on his ongoing popularity, even while behind bars, the attempt at understanding the Vybz Kartel phenomenon is part of the process of soul searching that is necessary for Jamaicans in this "season of fear".

Season of Fear

Nicholas Alexander is a high school teacher of literature and language; he won the Redbones Blues Café's Best Poet of the Year award in December 2014. (Redbones is a well-known jazz café in New Kingston, Jamaica.) His poem "Season of Fear" is a short free-verse piece of three stanzas and twenty-three lines with an uneven rhyming pattern, fast-paced continual movement and a mood of excitement heavily coated with dread/foreboding.¹⁰

> "Season of Fear"
> The Friday afternoon heats up
> to the pace of feet to and from work and school.
> The cup
> of life passed from weak to
> strong
> predicting Messiah's death so
> near
> in this season, sparking fear.

The golden glare of tropical
heat

is anything but the normal sign
associated with this day. Feet
frisk to their destiny – time
speeds up; tradition calling
a verdict cast, idols falling.
The men are quiet, music
none,
the faces pale though dark;
so frigid the rays of the sun
they seem to reflect the heart
of those mourning for their
king:
Not Christ but a Kartel of sin.

    The narrator tells of a Friday afternoon, which gets increasingly hot to the pace of feet as people move to and from school and work – quotidian practices. In the midst of the movement of the feet, another movement takes place: a cup – of life – passes from weak to strong and in the passing is the predicting of a death so near in "this season, sparking fear". The impending death predicted is of "Messiah" – unnamed, faceless and unknown. Perhaps we are immersed in the events of Good Friday, one of the most sacred days on the Christian calendar. Indeed, any mention of messiahs invariably brings to mind the Christian Messiah, Jesus the Christ, although messiah need not have religious overtones, but simply be reference to a zealous leader with a cause or an expected deliverer. This non-religious meaning may have relevance in exploring messianic Vybz as the Messiah, whose death is predicted, is not "a" or "the", simply "Messiah" (uppercase M).

    The movement continues in stanza 2 in "the golden glare of tropical heat", which is anything but "the normal sign associated with *this* day". (Which day? Friday? Another unnamed day?) The movement to destiny suggests some kind of judgement day – the judgement already predicted in stanza 1. Feet frisk to their destiny as time speeds up; the use of the word *frisk* to describe movement to destiny immediately suggests "patting down" and "body searches" - criminality and the realm of the gaol. The feet are clearly specific feet of someone, perhaps the accused, death-haunted Messiah, who has to face the tradition of the courts, calling. A verdict (guilty? death?), signalled in the first stanza, is cast and idols are falling. Here, the term *idol* carries the weight of both the religious condemnation of "lusting after other gods" and, ironically, the contemporary designation of popular artistes and movie actors as "idols".

In stanza 3, the movement indoors, signalled by "a verdict cast" in the preceding stanza, finds "the men" quiet, "the music none", "the faces pale though dark". There is a stillness resulting from the verdict cast; mourning is precipitated. Perhaps dismay, dread, fear have paled formerly dark faces. The rays of the sun are described paradoxically as so frigid they reflect the heart of those in mourning for their king. The frigid rays of the sun are a pathetic fallacy foreshadowing the grief of the king's followers/subjects. There is also something of an oxymoron in the phrase with the juxtaposition of frigid (as cold) and the rays of the sun (as warmth). The poem climaxes with the identification of that king by the placement of a strategic colon "king: not Christ but a Kartel of sin". "Kartel" begins with an uppercase K so there can be no mistaking the referent.

A Kartel of Sin

What on the surface appears to be a contemporary Lenten reflection on the passion (suffering) and death of Christ gets turned on its head in the final line of the poem and is shown to be a metaphor for the trial, conviction and sentencing of popular dancehall artiste Vybz Kartel (Adidja Palmer) and his four co-accuseds; ironically, perhaps a cartel of criminality or, in Alexander's eyes, "a Kartel of sin". The fact that "Vybz Cartel" was originally the name of a group, later appropriated by Palmer, when the members went their separate ways, may shadow this reference to Kartel the person and Cartel/Kartel as a group of co-accuseds. Lent was in full swing during the "season of fear", having begun on Ash Wednesday, 5 March 2014. Lent is the season when Christians, especially Roman Catholics, undertake penance, fasting and reflection. The forty days of Lent climax with the Eastertide resurrection of their Messiah, Jesus of Nazareth ("Christ" or "Messiah" means "anointed one"), on Easter Sunday: "So it is written that the Christ would suffer and on the third day rise from the dead" (Luke 24:46).

Alexander's message is in the metaphor, which is rife with Christian allusions such as "cup", "Messiah", "verdict", "cast[ing of lots]", "idol", "Christ", "sin". Such allusions are intelligible in the Jamaican space where most people consider themselves Christian, even if they do not attend church. Indeed, a *Gleaner* newspaper poll (17 February 2015) saw 83 per cent of Jamaicans claiming to be religious, that is, Christian. Biblical allusions and language are staples in Jamaican communication and the Bible is the standard of judgement for most things. As we will see later in this chapter, this has played out interestingly in the past in Jamaicans' choice of political leaders. In the case at hand, therefore, no eyebrows would have been raised when the senior deputy director of public prosecutions (SDDPP) Jeremy Taylor[11] ended his closing arguments at the trial with a verse from Psalm 37: "The Lord laughs at the wicked for He knows their day is coming" (verse 13, as reported by Barbara Gayle, *Daily Gleaner*, 21 March 2014). The SDDPP used this psalm effectively as it is a psalm that answers the question, "Why do the wicked prosper and the good suffer?" It takes no stretch of the imagination to identify who is identified as the "wicked" and who are perceived as the "sufferers". In Alexander's eyes, the wicked sin. Alexander renders his own verdict on Kartel/Palmer, perhaps a deeply theological verdict, as he charges Kartel with "sin". He calls Kartel out for sinfulness, a deeply Christian concept that, having rejected Euro-Christianity, Kartel would have been at pains to dismiss (Palmer and Dawson 2012). In the SDDPP's eyes, the promise of divine retribution against the wicked in the present is to be seen unfolding in the expected (predicted?) verdict of "guilty".

So, what appears to be an ordinary time for Jamaicans as they move between work and school is shown to be anything but ordinary as something extraordinary is afoot. It is also not an ordinary time on the liturgical calendar of the church as the season of Lent was being observed. And in this extraordinary time, one of the longest murder trials in Jamaican Circuit Court history is happening. The Kartel trial lasted sixty-five days and put on trial the very justice system and the justness of the aspirations of ghetto people for social and intellectual leadership, and for a "free[d] Worl' Boss", as Kartel is called by his fans. Some would say it was an extraordinary trial as it led to the conviction of a person of some standing in the Jamaican society, and this is not often the case.

The symbol of feet, which appears in the first two stanzas together, provides the sense of movement and urgency that ties the external quotidian space to the internal traditions of the courtroom. Simultaneously, perhaps it is also a plain sight reference to the "shoes" (slang for guns) that were lost leading to the murder of Clive "Lizard" Williams, Kartel's victim. Perhaps the movement of the cup of life from the weak to the strong signals the movement of the trial into the hands of the jury, who now have the power of life and death over the accused. Once upon a time, the accused were the strong, now made weak in the face of the tradition calling; the respected traditions of the courts have called Kartel and his co-accused to account. The world has been turned on its head, a reversal ensued.

At the same time, echoes are heard of Jesus's plea to God the Father in the face of crucifixion to "let this cup pass from me" (Mark 14:36). The cup shared at a table with his disciples on the previous evening as well as the drink offered to the Messiah on the Cross also shadow this image very closely. "This day" is the day of the verdict, a Thursday, when the accused have their date with destiny. The guilty verdict was handed down ("cast") on Thursday, 13 March 2014 – ostensibly the day of betrayal if we follow the biblical timeline leading up to the death of Jesus. The Kartel jury took less than two hours to render a verdict which did not change after the judge sent them back to reconsider. Jesus Christ is traditionally believed to have been crucified on a Friday, hence the Christian commemoration of the Friday which is called "Good" as a solemn day in the Easter Triduum of Holy Thursday, Good Friday and Holy Saturday (Matthew 27:27–28:8; Mark 15:16–16:19; Luke 23:26–24:35; John 19:16–20:30). Many of his supporters believed Kartel was betrayed by the justice system and his lawyers did argue that there existed a conspiracy to convict him. Kartel himself asserted that he was a victim of a conspiracy by the security forces. He boldly compared his travails with that of Jesus Christ, who was guiltless yet sacrificed by "Roman soldiers".[12] The previous day (12 March), numerous Gaza-ites (that is, Kartel's fans), including women and children, had taken to the streets with placards, chanting "Free Worl' Boss" and predicting that he would be freed (Bryan 2014).[13] On 3 April 2014, a sentence of life in prison was handed down for Kartel and three of his co-accuseds with Kartel to serve a minimum of thirty-five years before becoming eligible for parole. (The appeal of this sentence is set for July 2018.) In this regard, the guilty verdict foreshadowed the sentencing.

Predictions of a guilty verdict sparked fear in some social circles as to how Kartel's supporters, especially those in the Gaza (that is, his community of Waterford in Portmore, St Catherine), would react. Under state directives, the police took various precautions to prevent the violence that was predicted as potentially possible with heavy police presence, barricades, large water guns, disallowing media interviews of the crowd and urging Gaza-ites to leave the streets as some of their key strategies (Koch 2014). Interestingly, the expected eruptions did not occur and supporters outside the Courthouse in Downtown Kingston and in "Gaza" expressed shock, sadness, disappointment and surprise at the verdict. For many others, it was simply the expected verdict for someone whose class of origin lay in the real working classes from a poor community like Gaza in an unjust Jamaican justice system. In their eyes, once again, Messiah is unjustly convicted. It is ironic perhaps that the role of the messiah as one who suffers was totally missed in the Kartel story. Unlike for Kartel, the crowds called out against Jesus of Nazareth, "Crucify him! Crucify him!" Similarly, the ironies of his status as an idol, which is a false god and therefore to be utterly rejected in Christianity, is missed by his fans, some of whom, according to Thwaites (2014) set up "on Facebook, a page named 'Gaza Fans Only' advertised itself as, Made To Show Respect To Our Idol That Was Convicted By Jamaica's Corrupt System'". Once again, idols falling. (See Earl Lovelace's *While God's Are Falling*).[14]

Newspaper reports were that Kartel turned pale upon hearing the verdict being read, although Laura Koch (2014), *Gleaner* intern, reports him as looking pale before the verdict stating: "Adidja Palmer, popularly known as Vybz Kartel, was pale, as he and his co-accused entered the courtroom minutes after 5:30 p.m. yesterday. Kartel's eyes were half closed and he didn't say a word."

Of course, in the three years he had been incarcerated awaiting trial, Kartel had regained much of the dark colour in his complexion, not having regular access to his skin bleaching (lightening) products, such as the famous cake soap. (Cake soap is a type of laundry soap that Jamaicans claim helps to lighten the skin.) Kartel caused much controversy when he used products to lighten his skin ("bleach") and to publicly endorse this practice. In Jamaica, where the majority of persons are descendants of enslaved Africans and where issues of personal worth based on skin colour continue to be rife, Kartel's skin modifications caused consternation and generated controversial social debate. Kartel celebrated his skin bleaching in his music, for example, his hit song "Like a Colouring Book" (CD Empire Universe: The Second Chapter). According to Brown-Glaude (2013, 54):

> In the song, Kartel celebrates his tattooed body, which is covered with more than twenty-five tattoos. He bleaches his skin to highlight the tattoos and claims that his bleached, tattooed body makes him irresistible to women who now see him as "pretty". For Kartel, skin bleaching and tattooing are important parts of his "body work" for cosmetic purposes – i.e., to make him "pretty" – and has nothing to do with racial self-hatred or low self-esteem.

As such, there is a play on words, "pale though dark", where one is immediately reminded of Kartel's famous bleached and tattooed colouring book complexion and his role in sparking intense controversy around these aesthetic choices. (For more discussion on the Jamaican skin bleaching phenomenon, see also Charles [2003] and Hope [2011].)

In a *Reggae Times* review of *Voice of the Jamaican Ghetto*, which can be judged to border on the sycophantic, Jobson (2012) admits to minor discomfort with Kartel's bleaching: "Post-bleaching, Kartel appears viscerally stirring, pale and nearly unrecognizable compared to the burgeoning deejay on the cover of Up 2 Di Time. Yet for Kartel, bleaching is a practice of subversion that resists the panoptic surveillance of Babylon."

The group of artistes is silent and the music is silenced. The one, who has labelled himself "teacher ... dancehall artist/hero, businessman, proud father of seven children and counting ... new star ... not merely a DJ but a poet of Shakespearean stature" (Kartel 2011, 24, 26) and "voice of Jamaican Ghetto People" is silenced/silent in the face of the very system he indicted. Having referred to him as "Messiah" and "idol", perhaps Alexander's critique of the Kartel phenomenon resides in his leadership role – a role which Kartel, paradoxically, rejects as well as claims. In an interview with Winford Williams on the CVM TV programme *On Stage*, he rejects the status of role model for the youth of Jamaica – a status seemingly thrust upon him. Yet, he takes upon himself the role of being "the voice for the ghetto". In his 2011 University of the West Indies lecture, Kartel effectively deflected responsibility and social leadership stating: "Society wants Vybz Kartel and other entertainers to carry the weight of the social problems on [our] shoulders. [I am] an entertainer . . . if you want Vybz Kartel to play the role of a role model, then you have already lost as a parent" (Toppin 2011).

Yet he claimed that the more the media "gives it" to Vybz Kartel, the more the people view Kartel as a champion of their causes and embrace him because, after all, "what is an artist without the people" (Palmer and Dawson 2012, 27). Or what is a messiah without his faithful?

Messianic Leadership

In putting Kartel's messianic identity into context, it is necessary to look at political leadership in the Caribbean from as far back as before independence. The immediate pre-independence period in the Caribbean gave birth to a cadre of indigenous leaders "who possessed charismatic presence and oratorical ability and made use of, or alluded to, religious themes, especially the exodus story" in their claims of legitimacy and authority (Perkins 1995, 65). Such leaders felt "called" to lead mass movements of liberation for their people from beneath the yoke of oppressive colonialism ("Pharaoh/Egypt") into independence and nationhood ("the Promised Land").[15] This phenomenon has been variously described, including: "heroic" (Sunshine 1988; Singham 1968) and "charismatic" (Meeks 2000; Allahar 2001) and "doctor-politicians" (Burton 1997). Rex Nettleford (1993) characterized this type of leadership as "messianic", identifying the religious (Christian) framing of the Jamaican/Caribbean people as the most important factor in the shaping of this leadership type. Caribbean people in general, and Jamaicans in particular, are recognized as being deeply religious people with a strong religious consciousness such that Christian teachings are highly respected; most people tend to side with opinions expressed by the church, and people routinely use religious language and imagery while claiming religious warrants in all kinds of situations (Perkins 1995). Obika Gray (2004) describes the correlate of this as a political culture of political messianism among the people, which he judges as not having benefited them. Anton Allahar (2001) makes an association between times of crisis and the rise of charismatic leadership in the Caribbean region. The two or three turbulent decades leading up to independence, where, it can be argued, there was a concentration of such leadership in the region, was such a time. The two key Jamaican examples of messianic leaders are late prime ministers and cousins Alexander Bustamante and Norman Manley. For Jamaica, this style of leadership extended beyond independence with Michael "Joshua" Manley and his politics of change. Brian Meeks (2000) marks the death of Michael Manley in 1997 as the end of charismatic leadership in Jamaican politics.[16] Such types of leadership existed in tandem with informal leadership at the community level, which oftentimes performed an intermediary role between the leaders and their devoted followers. Among those forms of leadership, artists have always been held in high esteem, especially as they too demonstrated "the eloquence of the preacher and all the cunning of Anancy" (Burton 1997, 259). The question, therefore, arises: Who or what filled the space evacuated by the charismatic leader in the succeeding era, especially in the eyes of the ghetto people? Was it the originators of dancehall and artistes such as Vybz Kartel? In exploring the nature of stardom in Jamaica, Sonjah Stanley Niaah (2009) tackles the same phenomenon from a different but related angle. She asks, "What is it about the Caribbean populace, their life and style, which predisposes them to a consciousness of, search for, and manifestation of stardom?"(3). Stanley Niaah maintains that Jamaica/the Caribbean has its own understanding and manifestation of stardom. One can theorize that perhaps a space was opened up for other kinds of leadership to fill the gap on the national stage.

Some evaluations of the performance of post-independence leadership in Jamaica have judged it to have been at best middling with various leaders assessed as performing well in some areas and not so well in others (Jamaica Economy Project 2006). Indeed, part of the reason for this judgement is the argument that, post-1970s, the state became increasingly unable to provide the resources needed by various groups within Jamaican society, especially the urban poor. As a result, power shifted to politically aligned and criminally inclined community leaders, who were already central to a tribal way of distributing the resources of the state. Thus, "the don" or "area leader" becomes the source of welfare and largesse for masses of the urban population, who began to frame their moral behaviour in terms of what Obika Gray (2004) conceptualizes as "badness-honour". Gray (129) argues that such posturing was not unique to Jamaica, but is a rather mundane ubiquitous "weapon of the weak". He notes:

> Gestures of badness-honour may form the basis for a heroic individualism in contexts of deprivation. And while badness-honour is a form of personal charisma, it is surely the dark side of that magnetism. Indeed, where an optimistic populist charisma had once been the primary stock-in-trade of politicians and notables in Jamaica, that heroism was rapidly eclipsed in the post-war period by a snarling, violence-provoking disposition among both urban politicians and their ghetto supplicants. The former used violence-ridden histrionics to overawe and compel respect from boisterous, reckless supplicants; the latter embraced a similar aggression both as a mark of social distinction and as leverage on discriminatory political processes. (130)

Gray indicts the political culture that developed in the 1970s on the basis of Jamaica's infrastructural and sociopolitical heritage. The tendency towards personality political leadership and the inclination towards messianic forms of loyalty among political supporters helped engender a "violent winner-take-all political culture" (138).

In the Jamaican space, perhaps the most famous of such characters in recent times is Christopher "Dudus" Coke, who inherited his position from his father, Lester Coke. It is not a far throw to move to the badman deejay, who is a product of the inner city, the birthplace of dancehall, and who now has the popularity and resources to control the lives of entire communities. Indeed, Dennis Howard (2010) identified a long-standing connection between so-called badman artistes and area dons as well as political parties and politicians. In the early days of dancehall, the dons were in the forefront of the promotion of this new music form. Howard (2010, 13) says of the relationship between the two, "The relationship between artiste and don is a symbiotic one, which by its nature supports and promotes the criminal acts that are sometimes performed by these badmen/rudebwoys." Dancehall artistes were also themselves clearly politically aligned and the politicians supported their music and used it oftentimes during their campaigns. Michael Manley is said to have been the most successful at this.

Mavado and Vybz Kartel are perhaps the better known recent examples of such "badman DJs", who engage in very public feuds (McGlashen, n.d.). As previously noted, Kartel went so far as to assault veteran deejay Ninjaman on stage, perhaps in a bid to dethrone this longstanding dancehall Don Gorgon. Ninjaman, SuperCat, Josey Wales and Bounty Killer are other well-known examples of this type of deejay who have all had run-ins with the law with charges as varied as gun possession and murder while maintaining significant regard among their fans.[17] Hope (2006, 127) identifies these performers as belonging to a select group of artistes who have been linked to the promulgation and romanticization of violence stating: "Their allegedly close involvement with gun/violence in their real social relations, coupled with their role as dancehall artistes and cultural griots and deejays, means that while staging, exhibiting and embodying (gun) violence in the dancehall, these men are involved in producing meaning from social practices that form a part of Jamaican ghetto reality and dancehall worldview."

Kartel is alleged to have been involved in various criminal activities and was arrested and charged for Burton's murder before that of Clive Williams. He was subsequently acquitted of the previous charges. His song "Guns Like Mine", one of his numerous gun songs, is instructive:

> Dem nuh got no guns like mine
> no KG 9A copper shot a buss dem bighead and bruck spine
> Me sey one at a time bad bwoy form line
> Den beat carbine who nuh dead get blind
> Me have dem life pon line like clothes pon line
> Kartel buss one inna b—— bwoy spine.
> (Howard 2010, 13)

McGlashen (n.d., 8) argues that the persona of the badman artiste "is accepted and celebrated by some Jamaicans and has become normalized as a part of Jamaican reggae and dancehall music culture, which, by extension, is accepted in Jamaican culture as one way of being masculine and entertaining".

It can be argued that ghetto people see Kartel as a kind of saviour or charismatic figure – as a Messiah/Idol/Worl' Boss. Indeed, trial judge Justice Lennox Campbell acknowledged Kartel's popularity and the celebrity status that he had been accorded, "I suppose he's a celebrity of sort, so people will always be following him" (Vybz Kartel Trial 2014). Ironically, in the trial of

Jesus, it was not the Messiah who the crowds demanded to be released, but rather the bandit Barabbas. In fact, the crowd demanded that the Messiah be crucified. In contrast, Laura Koch reminds us that the crowds outside the court shouted: "Free Worl' Boss!" and even "Free world leader!"

Yet, it is not ghetto people alone who seem to revere Kartel. Well-known Rastafarian attorney-at-law Michael Lorne has stated, among other things, that "whether we like it or not, there is something phenomenal about Kartel" (Gayle 2014). Similarly, Jobson (2012) opines, "That a Society child now hangs on Kartel's every word speaks to the potential of a still unrealized project of decolonization, which as he observes, rests on 'Dancehall [as] one of the few places where uptown meets downtown on an even playing field'". Such claims make a case for the important political role of a messianic deejay, which echoes the role of former messianic leaders in postcolonial times. Indeed, there is much that is similar between Kartel's self-understanding and that of charismatic politicians of a previous age, so much so that lawyer-cum-journalist Daniel Thwaites (2014) describes Kartel as "well educated, skilful at public relations, and more charismatic than all but three or four of our politicians".

Messianic Vybz

Kartel's self-understanding is made evident in his co-authored book *The Voice of the Jamaican Ghetto*. The conversation begins with the image on the cover. Kartel is portrayed as a contemporary Malcolm X, including the eyeglasses, the contemplative pose and the ring on the fourth finger of his left hand. Interestingly, the ring on Kartel's finger appears to be a Masonic Lodge ring, since it bears the standard Freemason symbols of a square and compass combined. This, among other things, fuels the rumours that he is a paid up member of the Lodge who has sold his soul to the devil. In several interviews, Kartel has laughingly deflected questions around this issue. (Incidentally, Malcolm X's ring is a crescent moon and star, the symbol of the American Society of Muslims.) Kartel's Gaza tattoo on his fingers is also prominent. Among the resources listed at the end of the book is Malcolm X's "The Ballot or the Bullet" speech (Detroit, 12 April 1964). Therefore, it is unsurprising that the book sounds like much that we have heard before,

A KARTEL OF SIN? MESSIANIC DESIRES AND VYBZ

even as it proclaims itself to be delivering secrets Babylon does not want the ghetto people to know. Veteran journalist Barbara Gloudon's (2014) comment is therefore apt as she says, "Grazing through the pages of the book, I came to the conclusion that I'd been there before." Interestingly, after Kartel was found guilty, attorney Michael Lorne said it was unfortunate as "he [Kartel] had actually started reading uplifting material like the Autobiography of Malcolm X, The Philosophies and Opinions of Marcus Garvey, The Promised Key and books on herbal healing. He was also seriously considering stopping bleaching" (Walker 2014). Some of these readings may have been directed towards preparing *The Voice of the Jamaican Ghetto,* as echoes of these writings are present in the text. Yet, is worth considering why Kartel chose Malcom X as his model rather than, say, Marcus Garvey, with his universal appeal and his obviously Jamaican connections. Perhaps he is repackaging their messages for a new generation, one that is more willing to give messianic artistes a hearing.

In *The Voice of the Jamaican Ghetto*, Kartel (and his co-author) speaks in lofty tones from on high as he reveals "truths" that he claims were hidden from the black masses of Jamaica. This is not a new claim as one of the tropes coming out of the experience of enslavement and captured by the Rastafarians, for example, is the practice of Babylon to miseducate and deceive. Kartel addresses the oppressors of "my people" with the hope that their hearts may be touched "so that they may treat the poor with compassion" (Palmer and Dawson 2012, 1). Like his music, which forms the framework for the book, Kartel intends for his words to bring about structural change in the Jamaican society – for example, with helpers and gardeners treated more humanely, prison officials implementing more humane and positive procedures in jails, and Jamaican males taking time to understand their mothers and their baby mothers. So he also is addressing his "people" as he prays (2): "Most of all, may it [the book] be a source of motivation for my people, especially the young ones, as they find their way through life in this lovely place, *Xamaica* – its original name before the genocidal Christopher Columbus came to plunder and destroy an entire Amerindian people under the guise of Christianity." The book is rife with similar sentences, in which a variety of facts and opinions are strung together in a fashion that is often difficult to follow, but perhaps done with an attempt at erudition.

The work also addresses the "haters", those persons who thrive on showing hate towards, criticizing or belittling Kartel and his followers. Kartel even stoops to bless them – because "the Gaza nuh bad mind" (2). Like the continued third-person references, Kartel also personifies himself in the place he grew up in Waterford, St Catherine, or the Gaza, as he renamed it. He is Gaza and Gaza is him.

Kartel speaks of himself in the third person – "Vybz Kartel/Kartel" throughout the book, which has clearly benefited from research on various local and international facts to bolster his argument. The book even quotes from the Bible and he claims to have "put away childish things". Indeed, he references the Bible in his lyrics – for example, "Thank You Jah" opens with the first two verses of Psalm 127. Interestingly, he validates the scriptures, especially the Book of Proverbs, which he claims is written by Solomon, while rejecting the Psalms, because he says, "Babylon have us continuously singing Psalms while we could spend some of that time reading the book of wisdom sanctioned by Solomon" (3). Kartel claims that reading a chapter a day to keep the devil away means reading the Psalms, but he rejects doing that as "devil business". This sort of unclear and contradictory argumentation is present throughout the text. Like many Jamaicans, Kartel's (and his co-author's) understanding of the scriptures is fairly rudimentary and so, even his following the traditional attribution of Proverbs to Solomon while rejecting the Psalms, which are often attributed to the beloved King David, is puzzling and clearly arbitrary. Indeed, the fact that biblical scholarship recognizes both Proverbs and Psalms as wisdom literature, therefore, having a similar concern with how to live wisely in this life is indeed ironic in this instance.

Concluding Thoughts

The popularity of such figures like Kartel suggests that the messianic political leader may have been superseded by the messianic artiste, who now challenges "Babylon" instead of "Pharaoh", dispenses largesse (and lofty advice), while providing hope for "Ghetto People" that they too can acquire the material resources held by their saviour. It should be noted here that Bob Marley is perhaps the best known example of a messianic artist who has been described as the essence of a Jamaican icon and superstar by Frederick Hickling (2009, 25): "Bob Marley was a hero figure, in the classic mythological sense. His departure from this planet came at a point when his vision of One World, One Love – inspired by his belief in Rastafari – was beginning to be heard and felt." Not only among Jamaicans, but in societies as diverse as the Hopi Indians, Maoris in New Zealand and in parts of West Africa, "Bob is seen as a redeemer figure returning to lead this planet out of confusion".

Such a phenomenon of the messianic artiste, which can be seen to be a continuation of the exodus politics of the pre-independence Caribbean/ Jamaican period, emphasizes the role of the leader and dismisses the role of the people, who may be seen as dependents to be easily manipulated, especially by virtue of their religious faith, gullibility, cultural inclination to seek after a messiah and economic need. Such styles of leadership continue to support an excess of emotionality and fervour with little critical vision. In this regard, a person's material resources/possessions become perhaps the primary centre of value. This has been a situation bedevilling Jamaican society for a long time and is reflected in and reinforced by elements of dancehall culture. These and other concerns make messianism in its current form just as troubling as its previous incarnation.

Notes

1. See https://nationalgalleryofjamaica.wordpress.com/2015/11/27/explorations-iv-masculinities-opens-at-the-national-gallery-on-december-6/vermont-howie-grant-dancehall-artistesrgb/.
2. Sting is an annual dancehall show billed as "The Greatest One Night Reggae & Dancehall Show on Earth!". By 2016, it had been staged for thirty-two years but was not hosted that year. Instead, it was replaced by an invitation-only Celebration Party and Awards Ceremony on Boxing Day 2016, honouring various artistes who over the years had contributed to the success of the show. Sting was famous for lyrical "clashes" between dancehall artistes. The 2002 clash with Ninjaman and Kartel was planned and highly anticipated by the fans. It got out of hand, however, when members of Kartel's crew physically assaulted Ninjaman on stage. In the melee, several people were arrested. Kartel was forced to make a public apology and declare a truce with Ninjaman several days later at a press conference. "If all the gun talk and curse words in the man's songs hadn't

already labelled him a possibly 'dangerous' artist, the Ninjaman incident surely did"(https://www.allmusic.com/artist/vybz-kartel-mn0000261309/biography).
3. Buju Banton is one of Kartel's idols, hence the name chosen to pay homage to his idol.
4. It is reported that the feud was result of a collaboration with D'Angel, the former girlfriend of Bounty Killer, who subsequently married his arch-rival Beenie Man.
5. The empire disbanded in 2013. Several members of the empire were either fired or left at various points. Blak Ryno, for example, decamped after complaining of being beaten along with Gaza Kim.
6. Busta Rhymes was present in Jamaica providing Kartel support during his trial for murder.
7. Run-DMC did this for Adidas and Ghostface for Wallabees.
8. See Toppin 2011 for a critique of this engagement.
9. It should be noted that while in prison, he continues to release music, especially under the label of his babymother Taneisha "Shorty" Johnson.
10. Compare his title with the phrase "season of drear" in Owen Campbell's poem "Ubi Gentium" published in *Kyk-Over-Al*, ed. A.J. Seymour, 1952 (photocopy). Thanks to Nicholas Alexander for allowing me to reproduce his poem here.
11. Interestingly, Jeremy Taylor is the son of well-known Baptist pastor the Reverend Dr Burchell Taylor, now retired from Bethel Baptist Church, so his own roots in the interpretation of scripture would perhaps be quite strong. Taylor would therefore have been aware that his use of scripture would have resonated with the jury.
12. Kartel professed his innocence and wrote a poem encapsulating this that was sent to Carolyn Cooper, now retired professor of the University of the West Indies, Mona. It was published both in her online blog ("A Letter to Adidja 'Vybz Kartel' Palmer", 19 March 2012, https://carolynjoycooper.wordpress.com/2012/03/19/a-letter-to-adidja-vybz-kartel-palmer/) and in the traditional media (all errors in the original):

(A poem) Guilty before trial?
by A. Palmer
The police have found me guilty and i
haven't gone to trial yet,
but they spread propoganda on T.V. & internet
Dem a beat it in the people's mind
that i'm guilty and deserve death,
but the public knows how the police

operate, so mi nah fret.
So many people in court for allegedly
taking 4, 5, 6 pickney life,
So how they don't discuss that on
'CVM at sunrise'?
Allegations of extrajudicial killings
by security forces have already been issue,
but i've never seen them on t.v. so
much, talking about that, did you?
Me never kill nobody yet
but they say my music breeds crime,
that's why they're on my case they
want me imprisoned long time.
I am an artiste so i know things
will make the news,
but don't crusade this ungodly way to
distort people's views.
Mi swear my innocence before all
mankind and God,
why would i risk going to jail Leaving
behind 7 children, after mi nuh mad.
I am not the first man
The romans soldiers have sacrificed,
like me, that man was not guilty
That man was Jesus Christ.

13. Kartel grew up in Portmore, St Catherine, Jamaica, which he labelled as the Gaza, with all the connotations of being under siege. As noted previously, Gaza is positioned in opposition to Gully, which is the label for Cassava Piece, St Andrew, the home of Kartel's dancehall rival Mavado. The Kartel-Mavado rivalry spilled over into the society (and outside of Jamaica) with young fans taking sides and even getting involved in violent confrontations with each other.

14. Furthermore, an image of Kartel as Jesus was circulated online during his trial, which caused some outrage among Christians. For those familiar with Christian iconography the painting is very telling as it could be seen to be Kartel as *Pantocrator* – Almighty or All Powerful (one of the specific ways Jesus is portrayed). The artiste claimed, however, that "The painting is a recreation of Ingres's – Jupiter and Thetis" and was done before the trial. Ingres's por-

trayal can be clearly seen to be the inspiration for the Kartel depiction (http://www.artble.com/artists/jean_auguste_dominique_ingres/paintings/jupiter_and_thetis). See http://www.yardflex.com/2013/12/vybz-kartel-jesus-painting-angers-christ.html for a description of the Kartel image and comments from the artist.

15. Price (2014) would argue that this tradition fits well into a body of cultural beliefs and practices about black messianism, which evolved over the course of nearly two hundred years. The key group among whom this black messianism can be seen to be at play are the Rastafari, who believe Christ is embodied in Haile Selassie or that he is God incarnate.

16. Sonjah Stanley Niaah (2009, 4), citing Chris Rojek (2001) and John Frow (1998), notes that "the cultural function of the celebrity today contains significant parallels with the functions normally ascribed to religion.... Various figures and effects on their audiences have been ascribed godlike qualities or fame."

17. Kartel is by no means exceptional as a charismatic messianic artiste, as the discussion maintains. He fits well into the genre of badman artistes but is perhaps the most prominent within the current time. It is noteworthy that his idol Buju Banton is, at the time of writing, still imprisoned in the United States on drug charges. Buju is scheduled for release later in 2018. In some ways, Bob Marley is a more charismatic messianic figure without being associated with the sort of nihilism with which Kartel is identified.

References

Allahar, Anton. 2001. *Caribbean Charisma: Legitimacy and Political Leadership in the Era of Independence*. Kingston: Ian Randle.

Brown-Glaude, Winnifred. 2013. "Don't Hate Me 'Cause I'm Pretty: Race, Gender and the Bleached Body in Jamaica". *Social and Economic Studies* 62 (1–2): 53–78.

Bryan, Chad. 2014. "Verdict Saddens 'Gaza City' Residents. *Gleaner*, 14 March. http://jamaica-gleaner.com/gleaner/20140314/lead/lead31.html.

Burton, Richard. 1997. *Afro-Creole: Power, Opposition and Play in the Caribbean*. Ithaca: Cornell University Press.

Charles, Christopher A.D. 2003. "Skin Bleaching, Self-Hate and Black Identity in Jamaica". *Journal of Black Studies* 33 (6): 711–28.

Fernando, S.H. 2014. "Murder Dem: The Turbulent Saga of Reggae Stars and Violent Crime – Why Have so Many Prominent Jamaican Artists Been Killed or Incarcerated?". *Cuepoint*. 10 December. https://medium.com/cuepoint/murder-dem-the-turbulent-saga-of-reggae-stars-and-violent-crime-fce07efeadd2#.4duy308vi.

Gayle, Barbara. 2014. "World Boss' Says 'Nothing Can Happen to Him: Prosecution Tells Jury to Note Kartel's Arrogance". *Gleaner*, 21 February. http://jamaica-gleaner.com/gleaner/20140221/lead/lead4.html.

Gloudon, Barbara. 2014. "An Outbreak of Kartelitis". *Jamaica Observer*, 11 April. http://www.jamaicaobserver.com/columns/An-outbreak-of-Kartelitis_16451554.

Gray, Obika. 2004. *Demeaned but Empowered: The Social Power of the Urban Poor*. Kingston: University of the West Indies Press.

Helber, Patrick. 2012. "'Ah My Brownin' Dat!' A Visual Discourse Analysis of the Performance of Vybz Kartel's Masculinity in the Cartoons of the Jamaica Observer". *Caribbean Quarterly* 58 (2–3): 116–28, 179.

Hickling, Frederick. 2009. "The Psychology of Stardom in Jamaican Popular Culture: 'We Never Know Wi Woulda Reach Dis Far'". *Wadabagei* 12 (2): 9–39.

Hope, Donna. 2006. "Dons and Shottas: Performing Violent Masculinity in Dancehall Culture". *Social and Economic Studies* 55 (1–2): 115–31.

———. 2011. "From Browning to Cake Soap: Popular Debates on Skin Bleaching in the Jamaican Dancehall." *Journal of Pan African Studies* 4 (4): 164–93.

Howard, Dennis. 2010. "Dancehall Political Patronage and Gun Violence: Political Affiliations and Glorification of Gun Culture". *Jamaica Journal* 33 (1): 8–15.

Jamaica Economy Project. 2006. Draft final report. Typescript.

Jobson, Ryan. 2012. "Independence Dreams and the GazaDon: A Review of Vybz Kartel's *The Voice of the Jamaican Ghetto*". *Reggae Times*, September.

Kartel, Vybz. 2011. "Vybz Kartel: Pretty Like a Colouring Book?" *Jamaica Journal* 33 (3): 26–29.

Koch, Laura. 2014. "Kartel Looked Pale before Verdict". *Gleaner*, 14 March. http://jamaica-gleaner.com/gleaner/20140314/lead/lead3.html.

McGlashen, Georgette. N.d. "Badman or Badman-tu: Defining Badman Artiste through Popular Cultural Forms Reggae and Dancehall". Typescript. http://www.inter-disciplinary.net/critical-issues/wp-content/uploads/2013/04/McGlashen-up3_dpaper.pdf.

Meeks, Brian. 2000. *Narratives of Resistance: Jamaica, Trinidad, The Caribbean*. Kingston: University of the West Indies Press.

Nettleford, Rex. 1993. *Political Leadership in the Commonwealth Caribbean: Responsibilities, Options and Challenges at End of Century*. Kingston: School of Continuing Studies, University of the West Indies.

Palmer, Adidja, and Michael Dawson. 2012. *Vybz Kartel's The Voice of the Jamaican Ghetto*. Kingston: Ghetto People Publishing.

Perkins, Anna Kasafi. 1995. "Exodus Politics in the Pre-independence Caribbean". In *Celebration of Black History: GYRO Colloquium Papers*. Boston: Boston College.

Price, Charles. 2014. "The Cultural Production of a Black Messiah: Ethiopianism and the Rastafari". *Journal of Africana Religions* 2 (3): 418–33.

Singham, A.W. 1968. *The Hero and the Crowd in Colonial Polity*. New Haven: Yale University Press.

Stanley Niaah, Sonjah. 2009. Introduction. *Wadabagei* 12 (2): 3–8.

Sunshine, Catherine. 1988. *The Caribbean: Struggle, Survival, Sovereignty*. 2nd ed. Washington, DC: Economic Commission for Latin America and the Caribbean.

Thwaites, Daniel. 2014. "Free Worl' Boss?". *Gleaner*, 23 March. http://jamaica-gleaner.com/gleaner/20140323/cleisure/cleisure4.html.

Toppin, Danielle. 2011. "On Vybz Kartel, Social Leadership and Stolen Laptops". *Starbroek News*, 11 April. http://www.stabroeknews.com/2011/features/in-the-diaspora/04/11/on-vybz-kartel-social-leadership-and-stolen-laptops/.

Walker, Karyl. 2014. "The Rise and Fall of Vybz Kartel". *Sunday Observer*, 16 March. http://www.jamaicaobserver.com/news/The-rise-and-fall-of-Vybz-Kartel_16272473.

Vybz Kartel Trial. 2014. "Judge Instructions to Jury [Full Transcript]". Dancehallhiphop.com, 6 March. https://dancehallhiphop.com/2014/03/06/vybz-kartel-trial-judge-instructions-to-jury-ignore-lyrics-ask-if-lizard-is-dead/.

CONTRIBUTORS

DONNA P. HOPE is Professor of Culture, Gender and Society, Institute of Caribbean Studies and the Reggae Studies Unit, the University of the West Indies, Mona, Jamaica, and founder of the Dancehall Archive and Research Initiative. Her publications include *Reggae from Yaad: Traditional and Emerging Themes in Jamaican Popular Music*; *International Reggae: Current and Future Trends in Jamaican Popular Music*; *Man Vibes: Masculinities in the Jamaican Dancehall*; and *Inna di Dancehall: Popular Culture and the Politics of Identity in Jamaica*.

RACQUEL BERNARD is currently pursuing her PhD in musicology at the University of California, Los Angeles.

ROBIN CLARKE is Senior Lecturer and Public Relations Officer of the School of Performing Arts, Excelsior Community College, Kingston, Jamaica, and Adjunct Lecturer, the Institute of Caribbean Studies, the University of the West Indies, Mona, Jamaica.

CHRISTIAN EUGENIO LÓPEZ-NEGRETE MIRANDA is Founder and General Coordinator of the Rastreando el Reggae Collective, National School of Anthropology and History, Mexico City, Mexico. He is currently pursuing his PhD in ethonomusicology at the National Autonomous University of Mexico.

KLAUS NÄUMANN is Professor of Ethnomusicology, Martin-Luther-University of Halle-Wittenberg, Germany.

ANNA KASAFI PERKINS is Senior Programme Officer, Quality Assurance Unit, Regional Headquarters, the University of the West Indies, Jamaica. Her publications include *Quality in Higher Education in the Caribbean*; *Justice and Peace in a Renewed Caribbean*; and *Justice as Equality*.

www.ingramcontent.com/pod-product-compliance
Lightning Source LLC
Chambersburg PA
CBHW021833300426
44114CB00009BA/417